C000046396

VOLUME 25

LOCKHEED MARTIN
F-117 NIGHTHAWK

BY DENNIS R. JENKINS

specialtypress
PUBLISHERS AND WHOLESALERS

Copyright © 1999 Dennis R. Jenkins

Published by
Specialty Press Publishers and Wholesalers
11605 Kost Dam Road
North Branch, MN 55056
United States of America
(612) 583-3239

Distributed in the UK and Europe by
Airlife Publishing Ltd.
101 Longden Road
Shrewsbury
SY3 9EB
England

ISBN 1-58007-020-5

All rights reserved. No part of this book may be reproduced or transmitted in any form or by any means, electronic or mechanical including photocopying, recording or by any information storage and retrieval system, without permission from the Publisher in writing.

Material contained in this book is intended for historical and entertainment value only, and is not to be construed as usable for aircraft or component restoration, maintenance, or use.

Designed by Dennis R. Jenkins

Printed in the United States of America

Front Cover: *An F-117A approaches a tanker. Noteworthy are the open inflight refueling receptacle on top of the fuselage, and the deployed forward-looking infrared sensor ahead of the windscreen. (Lockheed Martin Skunk Works)*

Back Cover (left): *An F-117A deployed at Aviano AB, Italy, on 21 February 1999, just prior to beginning of the bombing of Serbia and Kosovo. (U.S. Air Force/SrA Mitch Fuqua)*

Back Cover (top right): *A model of HAVE BLUE during radar cross-section measurement testing on the RATSCAT range in New Mexico. Notice the radar absorbing "cones" on the ground under the model to absorb reflected microwaves so that they do not interfere with the measurements. (Lockheed Martin Skunk Works)*

Back Cover (bottom right): *Serbian television was quick to show the remains of 806 after it was shot down on 28 March 1999, marking the first combat loss of the F-117. These photos show various pieces of the aircraft at the crash site. (Internet Sources)*

TABLE OF CONTENTS

THE LOCKHEED MARTIN F-117 NIGHTHAWK

PREFACE

AUTHOR'S NOTES AND ACKNOWLEDGEMENTS

The F-117A has served one purpose extremely well. It has furthered the reputation of Skunk Works as the builder of mysterious secret aircraft. In all fairness, it's a well deserved reputation. The old Lockheed Advanced Development Company, which finally gave up and officially changed its name to Lockheed Martin Skunk Works, has developed and built at least three excellent aircraft (U-2, Blackbirds, and the F-117A) in total secrecy, all below budget and ahead of schedule. It is a truly amazing record.

The actual capabilities and reputation of the F-117A will be determined by historians at some future date. No doubt the aircraft has given the Air Force an introduction to what a "stealth" aircraft is capable of, and has allowed tactics and doctrine to be developed for their use. The most serious combat to date, the Gulf War against Iraq, proved they could be used extremely effectively. Their use during the Serbia/Kosovo campaign has been marred by the first combat loss, although exactly why the aircraft was lost is still unclear.

The HAVE BLUE demonstrators and F-117A represent a technology that is unlikely to be seen again. It was a "first generation" attempt at building a low observable aircraft. The limited capabilities of the available computers during the HAVE BLUE gestation period would not allow a "normal" aircraft to be modeled to determine its radar cross-section, leading to the unusual faceted design. Technological advances during the 1980s overcame this limitation, and allowed Northrop to accurately model the curving B-2 "stealth bomber," and both Lockheed and Northrop to simulate their Advanced Tactical Fighter (ATF) designs, which resulted in Lockheed being awarded the F-22 Raptor contract.

One of the best books so far on the F-117A development effort is *HAVE BLUE and the F-117A – Evolution of the "Stealth Fighter"* by David C.

The A-12 was designed with a reduction in radar cross-section as a requirement. The curvaceous chines were added late in development to further lower the RCS. (Lockheed Martin Skunk Works)

Aronstein and Albert C. Piccirillo, published by the American Institute of Aeronautics and Astronautics in 1997. Although the book is not particularly well illustrated and the quality of photographs is marginal at best, it is an excellent chronicle of the development of HAVE BLUE and the F-117A, and goes into significant detail on some of the technology and politics relating to the development effort. Jay Miller's *Skunk Works – The Official History*, Midland Publishing Ltd, 1995, is another good source of information on the F-117.

I would like to thank my friends Mick Roth and Tony Landis for their contributions. Denny Lombard at Skunk Works provided his usual terrific photographic support.

Dennis R. Jenkins
June 1999

Lockheed Martin won the Advanced Tactical Fighter (ATF) competition with their F-22 design. This will become the first truly first-line stealth fighter in the Air Force inventory since the F-117A was produced in too small a number to be considered "first line." Advances in computer simulation allowed Lockheed to use curves on the F-22. (Lockheed Martin)

The Skunk Works collection (clockwise from top center); SR-71 Blackbird, T-33 T-bird, U-2R (TR-1) Dragon Lady, F-104 Starfighter, F-117 Nighthawk, and F-80C Shooting Star. (Tony Landis)

Odd looking from any angle, the shape of the F-117A was dictated by one thing – a lack of computer power. The computers of the day simply lacked the capability to accurately produce radar cross-section models of curved surfaces, forcing Lockheed to design an aircraft that only used flat surfaces. Amazingly, it flies! (Skunk Works/Denny Lombard and Eric Schulzinger)

THE BEGINNING

*"I conceal my tracks so that none can discern them;
I keep silence so that none can hear me."*
– Sun Tzu, circa 400 BC

From 1915 to 1936, Robert Watson-Watt worked at the British Meteorological Office and Department of Scientific and Industrial Research. In 1919, he patented a microwave device designed for use in atmospheric studies. Subsequent developments improved the accuracy and sensitivity of the unit, and his 1935 patent was the technical basis for the British RADAR system that proved effective against German air raids during World War II. Even though a large number of scientists and engineers helped develop the system based on Watson-Watt's patents, the King decided that Watson-Watt was the principle inventor and knighted him in 1942.[1]

The term RADAR was originally an acronym for RAdio Detection And Ranging, but its use in modern English is as a word in itself, so it is no longer capitalized.

The operation of radar is conceptually simple: a transmitter generates radio waves, which are then radiated from an antenna. A target, such as an aircraft, that flies through this transmission reflects

This drawing illustrates the drastic reductions in radar cross-section necessary to significantly reduce detection range. Small reductions do not have much overall effect, although they can offer a tactical advantage under some conditions.

a small portion of this radio energy back to a receiving antenna. This return signal is received by an antenna, processed, and displayed to an operator. Thus, the presence of the aircraft is detected. Because radio waves travel at a known constant velocity, the speed of light, the target's range may be determined by measuring the time taken for a radio wave to travel from transmitter to target and back to the receiver.

The long-wavelength radar systems that were used to defend Britain from German aircraft during 1940-41 measured range accurately, but were much less accurate in measuring direction because the radiated beams were very wide. By reducing the wavelength of the radio waves

it became possible to build antennas to form narrow beams that could be rotated like the light in a lighthouse. Only when the aircraft lay within the beam would a radar echo be received, providing a fairly accurate indication of the bearing of the target. Originally the transmitting and receiving antennas were separate because the electronics of the day could not perform both tasks simultaneously.

During the early 1940s, switching methods were developed that allowed the same antenna to be used for both transmission and reception. In 1940, Sir John T. Randal and Henry A. Boot invented the cavity magnetron, a device for generating high-power microwave pulses. This invention transformed radar

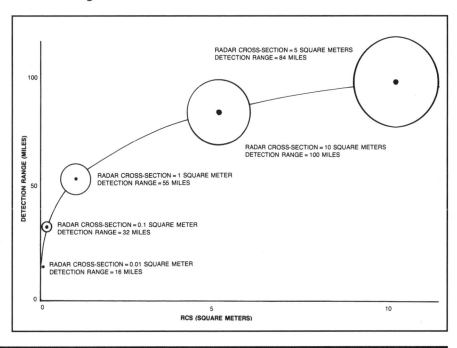

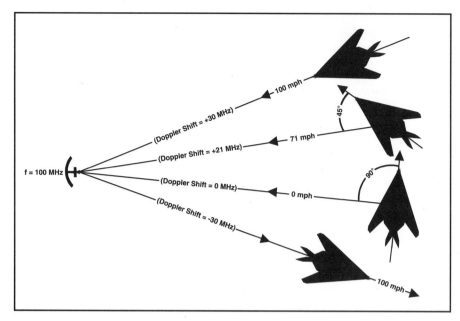

The Doppler theory states that a reflected microwave beam will incur a frequency shift based on the relative direction and speed of the target. If the target is moving away from the radar, the frequency will shift downward slightly. If the target is moving toward the radar, the frequency will shift upward. (U.S. Air Force)

units from large ground-based structures to fairly lightweight transportable units suitable for use on ships and aircraft. Compact S-band (10 cm) and X-band (3 cm) radars with beam widths of 1 degree or less were soon deployed for early-warning purposes. Similar radar was also used as an aid in blind bombing missions to delineate the ground beneath the aircraft, functioning as a navigational aid as well as a target identifier. Microwave radars were also important to the antiaircraft artillery units of the army, providing target detection and automatic firing of the guns. Similarly, radar became an indispensable aid to naval operations.

The great operational advantage of microwave radars during World War II was that they were relatively free from electronic countermeasures (ECM) by the enemy. Electronic warfare has now become a major threat to military radar sys-

tems, and modern radars have to be designed to reduce the effects of ECM. For example, antennas have been developed with increased resolving power but with very low side lobes so that active jamming cannot penetrate into the receiver as readily as with earlier systems. Simultaneously, the effect of passive jamming is reduced: the observation of false targets because of backscatter from "chaff" – falling clouds of scattered tinfoil strips – is reduced.

More modern radar also provides excellent moving-target indication (MTI) by use of the Doppler shift in frequency that a radio wave undergoes when it is reflected from a moving target. A target moving towards the radar will shift the frequency of the returned beam in one direction, while a target moving away from the radar will shift the frequency in the other direction. The development

of the modern computer has allowed an unbelievable amount of intelligence to be gained from the return radar signal. For instance, it is actually possible to count the rotation of fan blades in an aircraft engine, and to derive sufficient information from this to identify individual aircraft by their engine signatures (much as submariners can identify individual submarines by the sound signature of their propellers). This technique requires a significant amount of processing power, and is not widely used – yet.

The radar operator during World War II interpreted the radar returns on a simple cathode ray tube (CRT) that essentially presented a "blip" in the relative position of the target. A single radar could measure distance or altitude, but not both, so frequently each operator had two CRTs, one displaying range and the other altitude. Modern computers made possible much better interfaces, fusing the data from multiple radars onto a single display to provide very accurate position data for the operator. These same electronics made it possible for the radar data to be used by other computers directly, without the need for an operator interpreting the results.

The Beginning of Stealth

Interestingly, the first proposal for reducing the radar cross-section (RCS) of an aircraft came from none other than Watson-Watt, in 1935. The British government believed it had a significant lead in the development of radar and did not pursue Watson-Watt's ideas. But the Germans did. The Horten IX flying wing was designed around a composite sandwich skin that used a charcoal core intended to absorb most of the

radar energy instead of reflecting it back to a receiving antenna. Fortunately, the war ended before the Germans could perfect this concept, and the single prototype of the Horten featured more conventional construction. The overall shape of the aircraft, vaguely similar to the current Northrop B-2 Spirit, was not influenced by RCS reduction, and was a simple extension of a design that Horten had used on earlier sport aircraft.[2]

The *Kriegsmarine* did deploy a limited number of U-boats that had radar absorbing materials (RAM) wrapped around their snorkels and periscopes in an attempt to hide them from Allied ships and aircraft that were inflicting heavy losses in the North Atlantic. This RAM reportedly reduced their radar signature by about 70%.[3] Fortunately for the Allies, the effort came too late.

RAM was not a new concept, and does not owe its origins to RCS reduction efforts. Even in the late 1930s, RAM was available commercially and was used to line the insides of antenna pattern measurement facilities used by radio

antenna designers and manufacturers. The materials were available with excellent absorption properties over a large bandwidth, and were even comparatively lightweight and low cost. They did have a major drawback however. To achieve a significant absorption rate, they were frequently applied in layers several feet thick! They were also not terribly forgiving of extreme environmental conditions (heat, cold, wet, etc.), and were quite fragile, usually consisting of a foam-like substance. Clearly this would not work on aircraft.[4]

Many of the German scientists and engineers who had participated in the development of advanced RAM concepts were captured by the British, giving them a post-war lead in the technology. The British continued research into radar-defeating technology at a low level immediately after the war, and actually used some RAM on English Electric Canberra reconnaissance aircraft during the 1950s. The RAM, however, was heavy and was hard to fashion so that it did not detract from the aerodynamic performance of the aircraft,

so the British largely abandoned the research. Instead they concentrated on flying above the effective range of radar-guided weapons. The results of all the British research was compiled into the "Dawson Report" and turned over to the Americans during the early 1960s.

The Americans had not waited for the Dawson Report. During the early 1950s, the American Central Intelligence Agency (CIA) had initiated the development of the Lockheed U-2 reconnaissance aircraft. The aircraft was intended to fly so high that it would remain largely unseen by radar, and essentially invulnerable to interception by missiles or fighter aircraft. By the late 1950s, however, operational U-2 missions were being flown on a routine basis, and the ability of the Soviets to track the U-2 was alarming to all concerned. Lockheed began investigating means to reduce the U-2's radar signature, and Kelly Johnson developed various concepts, some of which were quite fantastic and of questionable value. Perhaps the most bizarre concept was to string wires of various lengths between the fuselage,

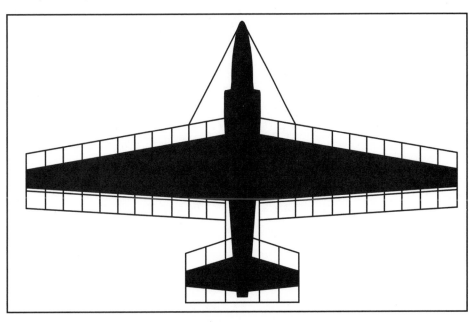

One of the more bizarre U-2 RCS reduction concepts was to string wires a quarter-wavelength away from the leading and trailing edge of the wing and tail surfaces. Ideally the return from the wire would cancel out the return from the edge since they were 180° out of phase with each other. Kelly Johnson revealed in 1975 that the flight testing of this configuration achieved "… negligible results in reduction of radar cross-section together with the expected adverse aerodynamic effects …" and the idea was dropped.

wings, and tail of the U-2 in order to scatter the radar energy in different directions. The concept was intended to counter relatively low frequency 70 MHz surveillance radars. Wires would be mounted a quarter-wavelength away from the leading and trailing edges of the wing and tail surfaces, so that the return from the wire would ideally be cancelled out by the return from the surface leading edge, being 180° out of phase with each other. Speaking at the 1975 Radar Camouflage Symposium, Kelly Johnson stated "The aircraft so equipped was flight tested with negligible results in reduction of radar cross-section together with the expected adverse aerodynamic effects …".[5]

The idea which was finally chosen for more extensive flight testing involved wrapping the entire airframe with a metallic grid known as SALISBURY SCREEN which was covered by a microwave absorbent ECHOSORB coating made of foam rubber (i.e., RAM). The resulting aircraft were often referred to as DIRTY BIRDS, and were almost universally disliked by pilots for their degraded handling qualities. However, none of the materials tested proved effective across the entire spectrum of Soviet radar frequencies, and all extracted a considerable penalty on aircraft performance. The coatings also prevented the dissipation of

The RCS of the U-2 was not considered during its design, mainly because very little serious thought had been given to the science of radar avoidance. The U-2's primary defense was its high altitude. However, as Soviet air defenses improved, Kelly Johnson began to investigate means to make the U-2 more survivable. One concept, applying radar absorbent foam over the entire outside of the aircraft, resulted in the so-called DIRTY BIRDS. (Lockheed Martin Skunk Works)

The closest U-2 is configured as a DIRTY BIRD with an ECHOSORB radar-absorbing coating over the entire exterior. This coating was not terribly effective, and also prevented heat transfer from the airframe, causing at least one in-flight accident, the loss of Lockheed test pilot Bob Sieker in Article 341. (Lockheed Martin)

The U-2 is probably Skunk Works most famous aircraft. Originally designed for the CIA, the aircraft was later purchased by the Air Force and is still in use 40 years later. Very little has been done to significantly reduce its RCS over the years. (Lockheed Martin Skunk Works)

heat from the engine through the aircraft skin. During a DIRTY BIRD test flight with the U-2 prototype (Article 341), Bob Sieker experienced a flameout at 72,000 feet due to heat build-up caused by the foam coating. Unfortunately Sieker's pressure suit faceplate failed and he suffocated before the U-2 crashed in the desert.[6]

Around the same time, the Air Force approached Teledyne Ryan to work on ways to lower the RCS of its highly successful BQM-34 Firebee drone. Teledyne Ryan fitted a wire mesh screen over the air intake and applied RAM to various locations on the airframe, resulting in a small RCS reduction from some angles. These techniques were used extensively on reconnaissance versions of the drones flown over Vietnam.

Further analysis by Johnson and Teledyne Ryan indicated that the only effective way to produce a smaller RCS was to design an aircraft with that objective from the beginning. About the only thing that

could be done for the U-2 was to paint it in such a way as to provide a small measure against being visually detected by fighters attempting to intercept during an overflight.

In 1956, the CIA appointed Richard M. Bissell, Jr., who had been the CIA's program manager for the U-2, to oversee the development of an advanced reconnaissance aircraft. Studies under the code name GUSTO investigated a new subsonic high-altitude aircraft that was designed from the beginning to be as invisible to radar as possible (the term "stealth" had not yet been applied to aircraft). Most of the Lockheed GUSTO designs took the form of large flying wings capable of altitudes in excess of 70,000 feet. Using then-existing material technology, it was quickly discovered that aircraft weight rose faster than its RCS got smaller. A new approach would obviously need to be found.[7]

In the fall of 1957 the CIA arranged for Skunk Works to determine how the probability of shooting down

an aircraft varied with respect to its speed, altitude, and RCS. This analysis demonstrated that supersonic speed greatly reduced the chances of detection by radar. The probability of being shot down was not reduced to zero, but it was evident that high speed overflight was worth serious consideration. Attention now focused increasingly on building aircraft which could fly at extremely high speeds as well as high altitudes.

Most tracking radars in the late 1950s swept a band of sky 30-45° wide and 360° in circumference. Any object in this area reflected the radar pulse in a manner directly proportional to its RCS. This return appeared on the radar screen as a spot or blip, and the persistence of this blip on the radar screen depended on the strength of the radar return, with blips from larger objects being brighter and remaining on the screen longer. During the late 1950s and early 1960s, a human operator watched the radar screen and kept track of the blips that indi-

The third A-12 (60-6926) shows the triangular panels used on the leading edges of the wings and chines. The chines were added very late in the design cycle primarily because testing revealed they would reduce the radar signature of the Blackbird. (Lockheed Martin Skunk Works)

cated aircraft within the radar's field of view. It was surmised that a high altitude object moving two to three times faster than a normal aircraft would produce such a small blip with so little persistence that a radar operator would have great difficulty tracking it, if indeed he could even see it. To take advantage of this it was determined that an aircraft must fly at approximately 90,000 feet and have an RCS of less than 10 square meters.

By the summer of 1959, both Lockheed and Convair had completed proposals for the new spy plane. Lockheed submitted a design for a ground-launched aircraft known as the A-11. The Pratt & Whitney J58 turbojet-powered aircraft would have a speed of Mach 3.2 at 90,000 feet, a range of 3,200 miles, and a first flight in January 1961. Kelly Johnson had refused to compromise the aerodynamics of this design in order to achieve a lower radar cross-section, and the A-11

presented a substantially larger target than a much smaller parasite aircraft being proposed by Convair, code-named FISH.

Convair's proposal depended on two high-risk factors. First and foremost was the unproven technology of the ramjet engines. Since ramjet engines had only been tested in wind tunnels, there was no available data to confirm that they would work in the proposed application. The second uncertainty was the B-58B bomber that was supposed to achieve Mach 2.2 before launching FISH above 35,000 feet, and was still in preliminary development and was not a confirmed or funded project.

Convair's proposal suffered a major setback in June 1959, when the Air Force cancelled the B-58B project and no other aircraft appeared capable of serving as a launch vehicle. The Convair proposal was therefore unusable, but the Lockheed

design, with its high radar cross-section, was also unacceptable. On 14 July 1959 both designs were rejected. Lockheed continued to work on developing a design that would be less vulnerable to detection, and Convair received a new CIA contract to design an air-breathing aircraft that would meet the general specifications being followed by Lockheed.

By the late summer of 1959, both Convair and Lockheed had completed new designs. Convair's entry was a delta-wing planform using stainless steel honeycomb skin and incorporating a crew capsule system which eliminated the need for the pilot to wear a pressurized suit. The Mach 3.2 KINGFISH had two J58 engines buried inside the fuselage, which significantly reduced the radar cross-section.

Lockheed's new A-12 entry was much like the A-11 but tuned to reduce the radar cross-section. A

small amount of cesium was added to the fuel to decrease the radar cross-section of the afterburner plume. In an effort to save weight Lockheed decided to use a titanium alloy to construct the A-12. Traditional lightweight metals such as aluminum were out of the question because they could not stand the heat generated at Mach 3.2, and steel was rejected because of its weight.

On 20 August 1959, Lockheed and Convair submitted their proposals to a joint Department of Defense, Air Force, and CIA selection panel. The two aircraft were generally similar in performance characteristics, but the Lockheed design was selected based mainly on cost. Ironically, the project to build the world's fastest aircraft was given the code name OXCART at the end of August 1959.

However, the selection panel remained concerned about the A-12's vulnerability to radar detection, and on 14 September 1959 the CIA issued a four-month contract to Lockheed to proceed with anti-radar studies, aerodynamic structural tests, and engineering designs. It was during this radar testing that the OXCART received its characteristic cobra-like appearance. Lockheed came up with a theory that a continuously curving airframe would be difficult to track because it would present few corner reflections or sharp angles from which radar pulses could reflect (this is, interestingly, exactly the opposite of the theory that led to the straight-edged F-117).

To achieve this, curved extensions were added to the engine housings and leading edges of the wings, and eventually to the fuselage itself, creating a large chine on each side. At first Johnson was concerned that these additions might impair the airworthiness of the plane, but wind tunnel testing determined that the chines actually contributed a slight aerodynamic benefit. Because titanium was very brittle and therefore difficult to bend, the necessary curvature was achieved by combining small triangular-shaped pieces of titanium that were glued to the airframe with a special epoxy adhesive.

Only the first A-12 used the titanium chine fillets; all later Blackbirds used fillets and wing leading edges made from electrically resistive honeycomb plastic with a glass-fiber surface that would not melt at high speed. When struck by a radar pulse, the composite chines tended to absorb the pulse rather than reflect it. The greatest remaining area of concern in the A-12's radar cross-section was the two vertical stabilizers. To reduce radar reflections, Kelly Johnson canted the stabilizers 15° inward and fabricated them out of resin-impregnated high-temperature plastic materials. The only metal in each vertical stabilizer was a stainless steel pivot. The Air Force, which later ordered two versions of the OXCART aircraft for its own use, was reluctant to use the laminated vertical stabilizers and generally flew with titanium ones instead.

The A-12 was the first serious attempt to build an operational aircraft with a reduced radar cross-section. In comparison to other aircraft of its era it was very successful. But radar technology was progressing rapidly, and the advent of more capable computers would quickly overcome whatever advan-

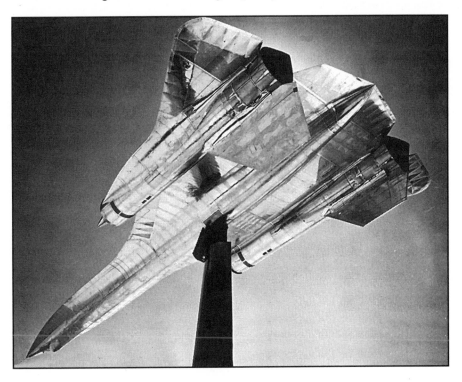

The A-12 underwent radar cross-section measurement testing during its development cycle, being amongst the first aircraft to do so. At various times both sub-scale and full-scale models were tested at several locations. (Lockheed Martin Skunk Works)

This is the mockup Q-21 drone, which was essentially identical to the production D-21 TAGBOARD drones that were used operationally for a brief period in the late 1960s. The D-21 had the lowest radar cross-section of any operational aircraft built until the advent of the SENIOR TREND aircraft. (Lockheed Martin Skunk Works)

tage the A-12 might have had when it was developed. The ultimate development of the basic A-12 shape, the D-21 drone, incorporated even more RAM into the design and was considered the "stealthiest" aircraft of its era (even though the term still did not exist at the time).

There were other attempts to produce vehicles with a low RCS. In 1962 the entire fleet of North American AGM-28 Hound Dog missiles were fitted with revised air intakes made of radar absorbent structures and covered with RAM. Reportedly this effort was very suc-

cessful in reducing the frontal RCS of the missile, which had a fairly low RCS just by virtue of its basic shape (no canopy, sharply swept wings, etc.). This is by all accounts the most successful of the "retrofit" RCS reduction efforts.[8]

Teledyne Ryan got back into the act in 1966 with the AQM-91A COMPASS ARROW high-altitude reconnaissance drone. Because its mission involved high-altitude flight, particular attention was paid to reducing the RCS of the drone as seen from below. The vertical stabilizers and sides of the fuselage were canted inward to

eliminate specular reflections from the side aspect or below the horizontal plane. The engine inlet was located above the fuselage and lined with RAM. The exhaust nozzle was also located on top of the fuselage to obscure it from below, and cooling air was mixed with the exhaust to lower the infrared (IR) signature. RAM was also applied to the wing leading edge and to some fuselage panels near the wing junction. Although the design was moderately successful at reducing the drone's RCS, it also revealed that a conventional wing-body design would probably never truly be "stealthy."

[1] Michael H. Carpentier, *Principles of Modern Radar Systems*, 1988. [2] David C. Aronstein and Albert C. Piccirillo, *HAVE BLUE and the F-117A – Evolution of the "Stealth Fighter"*, American Institute of Aeronautics and Astronautics, Reston, VA, 1997, p 195. [3] *Ibid*, p 196. [4] W.F. Bahret, *Introduction to Radar Camouflage* in the *Proceedings of the 1975 Radar Camouflage Symposium*, AFAL-TR-75-100, December 1975. [5] David C. Aronstein and Albert C. Piccirillo, *HAVE BLUE and the F-117A – Evolution of the "Stealth Fighter"*, American Institute of Aeronautics and Astronautics, Reston, VA, 1997, p 196. [6] Dennis R. Jenkins, *Lockheed U-2 Dragon Lady*, Warbird Tech Volume 16, Specialty Press, 1998. [7] Dennis R. Jenkins, *Lockheed SR-71/YF-12 Blackbirds*, Warbird Tech Volume 10, Specialty Press, 1997. [8] David C. Aronstein and Albert C. Piccirillo, *HAVE BLUE and the F-117A – Evolution of the "Stealth Fighter"*, American Institute of Aeronautics and Astronautics, Reston, VA, 1997, p 197.

HAVE 2 BLUE

In 1974, the Defense Advanced Research Projects Agency (DARPA) requested several aerospace contractors to study what RCS reduction was necessary to ensure the survival of an aircraft in a high threat environment. Fairchild-Republic, General Dynamics, Grumman, McDonnell Douglas, and Northrop were asked to participate, although Fairchild and Grumman declined due to a shortage of available engineering resources. General Dynamics reported that it did not believe RCS reduction alone could achieve the results the agency was looking for and asked DARPA to consider active ECM along with RCS reduction.

DARPA was unwilling to compromise and General Dynamics bowed out. This left just Northrop and McDonnell Douglas, both of whom were issued $100,000 study contracts. Hughes Aircraft, which contrary to their name did not build aircraft, but rather the radar systems that equipped them, was also funded to evaluate various aspects of the study. These initial studies were classified confidential, the lowest of the three current Department of Defense security levels (confidential, secret, and top secret).

It should be noted that the magnitude of the problem was large. In order to reduce the detection range by a factor of 10, the RCS of the target has to be reduced by a factor of 10,000. Previous efforts had managed RCS reductions of less than 50% – barely noticeable in real terms.[1]

Lockheed had not been asked to participate simply because nobody thought the company was still in the tactical aircraft business. The F-104 was the last production fighter that had been made by Lockheed, and production had ended almost 10 years earlier. But when Kelly Johnson found out about the studies, he approached the CIA for permission to brief DARPA on some of the RCS-reduction techniques tried on the U-2 and A-12. Since the aircraft were public knowledge by this time, the CIA voiced no particular objections, and DARPA soon included Lockheed in the studies.

McDonnell Douglas was the first competitor to publish a report detailing the RCS value necessary to defeat most surveillance radars, values later validated independently by Hughes. This was not surprising since McDonnell Douglas had already conducted some classified research for the Office of Naval Research (ONR) during 1973 on a "Quiet Attack" aircraft. This was probably the first serious attempt to design a "stealth" aircraft, although in this case the term was not limited to radar evading technology.

The Quiet Attack aircraft was a joint effort between McDonnell Douglas and Teledyne Ryan, with the latter bringing its expertise in low-RCS unmanned vehicles that were used extensively over Vietnam. The design had a maximum speed of 430 knots, but was optimized to fly

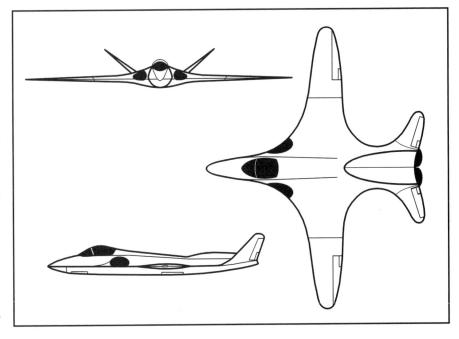

McDonnell Douglas designed a "Quiet Attack" aircraft for the Office of Naval Research during 1973. This experience did not appear to help the company during the HAVE BLUE competition. Unusually, the Quiet Attack aircraft was designed to fly at very slow speeds. (McDonnell Douglas)

undetected at about 110 knots. The visual signature was reduced by the use of airframe-mounted[2] "Yehudi Lights" intended to mimic ambient lighting, and the IR signature was reduced through the use of a novel exhaust nozzle for the single turbojet engine. The aircraft was vaguely reminiscent of the P-80 in plan view, but incorporated a constantly curving outline, a blended wing-body, and a butterfly-like empennage. RAM was used in some areas to further reduce the radar signature.

The constantly curving airframe, using much the same logic that Lockheed had used on the A-12, significantly reduced the RCS, but the fact that a small edge was always perpendicular to the incoming radar ensured that a small return was always generated. McDonnell Douglas intended to use active jamming to counter the small perpendicular return. The Navy considered this a fair tradeoff, although in the end the Navy elected not to pursue development of the aircraft. DARPA, on the other hand, was less interested in visual signature reduction, and flatly rejected the use of active jamming.

Lockheed and Northrop took a different approach. Lockheed's design was based on the results of some very obscure formulae that had originally been devised by Scotsman James Clark Maxwell and German Arnold Johannes Sommerfield in the early 1900s to predict the way any given geometric shape would reflect microwave energy. The formulae went largely unnoticed until 1962 when Piotr Ufimtsev, Chief Scientist at the Moscow Institute of Radio Engineering, used them as the basis for an openly-published paper on calculating the radar return of a two-dimensional

object. Although the paper was seemingly ignored by Soviet aircraft designers, Denys Overholser at Skunk Works decided that it offered a way to assist in designing a low-RCS aircraft.

Although the formulae were capable of predicting the effects for constantly curving structures, the computers at the time could not handle the enormous number of calculations necessary within a reasonable period of time. Overholser decided to break down the aircraft into a series of flat panels since the computers could handle the relatively small number of calculations. This gave birth to the multi-faceted design for the HAVE BLUE and F-117. Within a few years, there had been significant advances in computer technology which allowed Northrop and McDonnell Douglas to use continuously curving designs for the B-2 and A-12.

Even before discovering Ufimtsev's paper, Overholser had already decided that a multi-faceted design offered the most immediate way to reduce the RCS of an aircraft. Together with Bill Schroeder, Overholser developed the ECHO 1 computer program (the first of a long series of ECHO programs), and then used Ufimtsev's formulae to refine it. This program allowed the designers to orient the aircraft's facets to achieve the lowest possible RCS for certain angles.

It should be noted that computer programs of the day were run on large mainframes, and the primary method of data entry was punched cards. The entire aircraft design was reduced to several thousand punched cards and input through mechanical card readers. Every time the design

changed, a new card deck had to be punched. Output was largely tabular lists of numbers on continuous form computer paper, not graphical displays on monitors.

Foremost, Overholser and Schroeder were concerned with reducing the head-on RCS to minimize the possibility of detection while ingressing to a target.[3] The individual surfaces and edges were oriented in such a way as to reflect microwave energy into narrow beams away from the original source.[4] If each small flat surface could be angled differently in such a way that it would reflect energy away from the transmitter, the overall radar signature of the entire aircraft should be quite small.

After a great deal of experimentation, Lockheed determined that the optimum shape was a beveled diamond, which was quickly dubbed the "Hopeless Diamond" since it was aerodynamically impossibly to fly. Insiders have claimed that the Hopeless Diamond had an RCS 1,000 times less than the D-21.

But the world's least visible aircraft was worthless if it could not fly. Lockheed set about making modifications to the design such as slimming down the outer portions of the aft edges to become small wings, creating the notched delta planform later used on the HAVE BLUE demonstrators. Two vertical stabilizers, severely canted inward to the point that their tips almost touched, were added to improve directional stability. The problem with all of this was that the ever increasing number of facets quickly overloaded the ECHO program, forcing programmers to constantly revise ECHO to keep up with the design team.

On 1 November 1975, Lockheed and Northrop were selected for Phase I of the Experimental Survivable Testbed (XST) program.[5] This would involve building full-scale models of their designs for testing at a radar measuring facility, designing an actual flight vehicle, flight control simulation, and wind tunnel testing.

Full-scale model testing was not a new concept. It had been accomplished on various members of the Blackbird family in order to tune their RCS signatures, and everybody thought they understood the limitations of the available facilities. They were wrong. Both contractors were allowed to conduct model testing at the Grey Butte Microwave Measurement Facility run by McDonnell Douglas. This was the most capable measurement facility in the United States at the time, and had also been used for some testing of the D-21 and Teledyne Ryan drones. When the Lockheed and Northrop models were first tested, neither was visible. Instead the measuring devices were overwhelmed by the reflections from the pole the models were installed on. The fact that the same poles had been used in earlier tests and had not presented a significant problem simply serves to underscore the order of magnitude reduction achieved by the new designs. Lockheed provided a design to a low-signature pole that

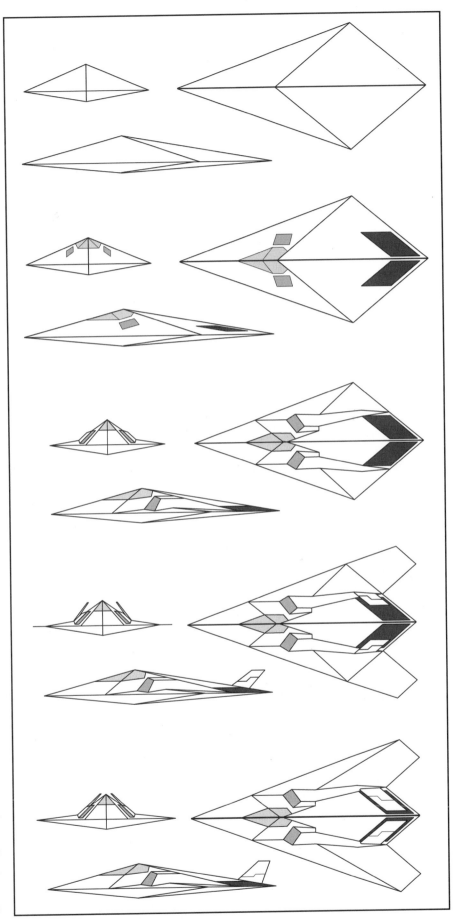

Conceptual drawings of the evolution of the ideal "Hopeless Diamond" (top) to a configuration generally similar to the HAVE BLUE demonstrators. These are based on conversations with Lockheed engineers and data provided in Aronstein's and Piccirillo's book.
(Dennis R. Jenkins)

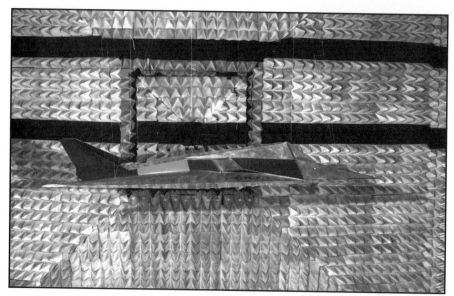

An early scale model of the HAVE BLUE is tested in Lockheed's anechoic chamber at Rye Canyon. The cones covering all of the walls, floors, and ceiling absorb stray energy to allow accurate measurements. (Lockheed Martin Skunk Works)

all three contractors agreed would probably be adequate, while Northrop provided a design for a mounting system. Simply because it seemed (rightly so) that Lockheed was in the best position to manufacture the pole quickly, they were allocated an additional $187,000 to provide a single pole which McDonnell Douglas would install at Grey Butte.

When DARPA finally released the criteria on how they would measure the RCS of the competing designs, Lockheed saw a small but significant loophole. Signature values at different frequencies and aspects would be multiplied by weighting factors, then added together – a common enough way to keep score. But the highest weighting factor was applied to the frontal aspect, with the rear and sides receiving almost negligible weighting. Lockheed carefully tuned the evolving Hopeless Diamond shape to deflect as much energy sideways and rearward as possible. Largely

this involved ensuring the leading edge and trailing edge sweep was as severe as possible – even if it compromised the controllability of the design.

Northrop also had a computer program (GENSCAT) that assisted in determining the RCS, and it too was largely limited to using flat surfaces. But unlike Lockheed's ECHO, GENSCAT *could* work on curved shapes, although the cost in computer time was significant, somewhat limiting its usefulness. This allowed Northrop to incorporate some curving shapes into the design, producing a design that looked a great deal more like a conventional aircraft. GENSCAT also formed the basis of the predictive tools that would eventually produce the B-2 stealth bomber.

In the end, the Northrop design was a faceted aircraft that looked much like the Lockheed entry. However some parts of the planform had slightly rounded edges,

and the air intake and exhaust were a continuously curving structure mounted on top of the fuselage beginning behind the cockpit.

The final tests revealed that Lockheed's design enjoyed a slight edge over the Northrop design from most directions, including the all important frontal aspect. In itself it was probably not enough to swing the decision, but combined with Skunk Works' known track record with "black" (secret) projects and experience with advanced composite materials, there was a consensus that Lockheed was most likely to succeed. In April 1976, Lockheed was declared the winner of Phase I and was awarded a $19.2 million Phase II contract to cover the detailed design and manufacture of two HAVE BLUE flight demonstrators. Lockheed would contribute up to $10 million of its own money to the program (Northrop had agreed to do the same should they have won). In the end, HAVE BLUE would cost a total of $43 million; $10.4 million from Lockheed and the rest from the U.S. Government.

Program management for Phase II was transferred from DARPA to the Air Force, which promptly imposed a "special access required" classification on the program, meaning that very little of the project would be known outside of those people directly involved. Even budget requests would be hidden in such a manner that the majority of Congress and the Office of Management and Budget would not know the HAVE BLUE demonstrators were being developed. Special access is above and beyond the normal three-tier classification levels, and essentially these programs do not exist except to a very few

people. There have been indications that the special access restrictions were actually put in place very late in the Phase I program.

Northrop's efforts were also seen to have promise. DARPA subsequently awarded Northrop a contract to design a Battlefield Surveillance Aircraft, Experimental (BSAX) that led directly to the TACIT BLUE stealth surveillance prototype. This aircraft provided some valuable data for the B-2 program and managed to remain completely unknown until the aircraft was turned over to the Air Force Museum in 1996.

HAVE BLUE Demonstrators

The word demonstrator is important. HAVE BLUE was never intended to produce an operational aircraft, or even a true prototype of one. The project was meant simply to demonstrate the concept of radically altering an aircraft's shape to achieve a significant reduction in RCS. A second objective was to prove the aircraft could fly. Minor objectives included validating existing modeling techniques and developing improved modeling techniques for use in future projects.

To build the two flight vehicles at a reasonable cost, the Lockheed prototypes would not be equipped with any operational equipment (weapons, fire control systems, etc.) and would use as many "borrowed" subsystems as possible. One aircraft was intended primarily as an aerodynamic demonstrator that would prove the flying qualities of the design, while the second aircraft would be complete with all the RAM and other tweaks deemed necessary to achieve the lowest possible RCS.

The modified "Hopeless Diamond" design served as a basis for the HAVE BLUE demonstrators. Engine intakes were located on top of the shape, covered with metal mesh grids that appeared solid to microwave energy. This allowed the ECHO program to deal with them as if they were simply another faceted surface. Subsystems "borrowed" from other programs included an undercarriage from the F-5E, non-afterburning 2,950 lbf General Electric J85-GE-4A engines from the Navy T-2C, and small items from a variety of other Air Force aircraft such as the F-15 and F-111. The cockpit was unpressurized, and an ejection seat from the YF-16 was used.

Neither aircraft was assigned an Air Force serial number and were known internally as HB1001 and HB1002. The demonstrators were 47.25 feet long, 7.5 feet high, and had a wingspan of 22.5 feet. Total wing area was only 386 square feet, but the effective lifting surface was much greater since the blended fuselage also generated lift at most attitudes. The structure was mostly aluminum, but some steel and titanium were used in high-heat areas. Zero fuel weight was 8,950 pounds, and 3,500 pounds of fuel could be carried. Gross weight varied between 9,200 and 12,500 pounds.[6] The first aircraft was painted an unusual multi-colored "disruptive" camouflage scheme intended to

A model of HAVE BLUE during radar cross-section measurement testing on the RATSCAT range in New Mexico. Notice the radar absorbing "cones" on the ground under the model to absorb reflected microwaves so that they do not bounce back from the ground and interfere with the measurements. (Lockheed Martin Skunk Works)

The second HAVE BLUE demonstrator in flight. Note the forward-retracting blade antenna under the forward fuselage. Also of interest is the extreme amount of faceting of the entire lower fuselage, which has a much deeper "V" than the later SENIOR TREND aircraft. The aircraft flew without any markings. (Lockheed Martin Skunk Works)

disguise its multi-faceted shape. The second aircraft was painted an overall light gray.

The aircraft was directionally unstable, so a fly-by-wire control system from the YF-16 program was installed. However, the control laws had to be modified to handle an aircraft that was unstable about all three axes (the F-16 is unstable only about the pitch axis). In fact, the HAVE BLUE control laws were never thoroughly developed since the aircraft was not meant to become operational. This somewhat limited the aircraft's maneuverability during the flight test program, but at no great loss to the tests being conducted. Like many other fly-by-wire aircraft of the period the control surfaces were commanded electrically via the computers, but the actual power to move them was hydraulic.

The modified delta planform had a leading edge sweep of 72.5° and did not incorporate flaps, slats, or other high-lift devices. In fact, the only control surfaces were two all-movable vertical stabilizers, inboard elevons, and an aft fuselage body-flap called a "platypus" that was automatically lowered whenever the angle-of-attack exceeded 12°.

The engine exhaust nozzle was also driven by RCS requirements. To prevent radar from seeing up into the engine, which was highly reflective, the tailpipe transitioned from the traditional round duct to a 17:1 flattened slot convergence nozzle. The trailing edge of each nozzle was angled 54°, corresponding to the airframe aft closure. This gives the appearance that the aircraft did not have an engine exhaust. A series of vanes at the trailing edge of the nozzle straightened the exhaust flow back along the longitudinal axis of the aircraft. The lower edge extending significantly further aft than the upper edge to help shield the IR plume. The designers also routed some engine bypass air around the tailpipe and nozzle to cool it, further reducing the IR signature in the process.[7]

A one-third scale model of the HAVE BLUE shape was tested at Grey Butte in December 1975, and an even smaller model found its way into the Lockheed Anechoic Chamber around the same time.

The results were encouraging, but the designers decided to tweak the design some more over the Christmas break. A second set of one-third scale model tests was conducted at Grey Butte in early 1976, for a total of 88 days of testing at the facility. After these RCS tests, a set of wind tunnel models was constructed to determine the basic aerodynamics of the shape. The low- and high-speed wind tunnel tests lasted only 1,920 hours, and confirmed the aircraft could fly, although it was truly unstable along every axis. This was not a direct result of the faceting but was linked to the large sweep angle on the wing which moved the center-of-gravity very far aft.

A full-scale RCS model was tested at the Air Force RATSCAT Backscatter Measurement Range at White Sands, New Mexico, and provided the final details necessary to begin construction of the two demonstrator aircraft. A total of 40 test days were used at RATSCAT.

By November 1977, the first aircraft had been completed and powered up inside the hanger at Burbank where it was built. Interestingly, when an aerospace machinist strike threatened to delay the completion of the aircraft, Lockheed managers took over and completed the aircraft on schedule. In order to run the engines as final checks, the aircraft was taken outside the night of 4 November and surrounded by large trucks, shielding it from any potential prying eyes. When everyone was satisfied, the aircraft was partially disassembled, loaded into a Lockheed C-5A on 16 November, and transported to the CIA's old U-2 base at Groom Lake, north of Las Vegas.

Once at Groom Lake, the aircraft conducted four low- and high-speed taxi tests. During the third test the aircraft's brakes overheated, a problem that would persist throughout the flight test program. It had only been 20 months since Lockheed had been awarded the HAVE BLUE contract.

The aircraft made its maiden flight on 1 December 1977, piloted by William M. "Bill" Park. The two J85s did not really provide sufficient power for the rather heavy demonstrator (which had an effective thrust-to-weight ratio of only 0.4:1), and its aerodynamic performance was moderate, at best (an L/D of 7.5, compared to 9-12 for a normal fighter). The aircraft was limited to load factors of +3/-1g (compared to +9/-5 for most modern fighters), and its maximum altitude was only 25,000 feet.[8]

Nevertheless, the aircraft quickly proved that the basic shape could fly successfully. For a bit of added safety while opening the flight envelope, the first aircraft had a spin recovery parachute installed on the upper aft fuselage (this is a relative term, given the shape of the aircraft), and featured a long flight test instrumentation boom on the nose.

Air data was sensed by a series of flush pressure ports on the upper and lower surfaces of the forebody, and three probes: one on the tip of the nose and two on the windscreen center frame. Data from these ports was compared to data gathered by the nose probe (which had more traditional instrumentation) and used to program the flight computers. However, the number and location of the flush data ports was not adequate for determining pitch and yaw angles accurately, and in the end inertial data from gyros and accelerometers was used instead.

Flight tests of the HAVE BLUE initially went fairly smoothly, and the fly-by-wire system functioned well. The landing speed was quite high (160 knots), as expected because of the lack of flaps or speed brakes. However, during the aircraft's 36th flight, on 4 May 1978, HB1001 landed excessively hard, jamming the right main landing gear in a semi-retracted position. Bill Park pulled the aircraft back into the air, and tried to shake the gear back down. After his third attempt failed, he took the aircraft up to 10,000 feet and ejected. Park hit his head on the way out of the aircraft and was knocked unconscious. Unable to control his parachute during land-

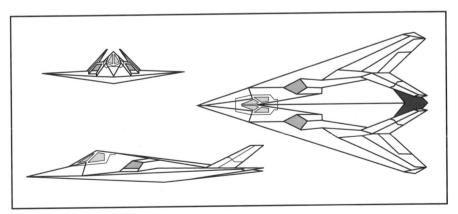

The Final HAVE BLUE shape. (Lockheed Martin Skunk Works)

and all gaps had to be filled in with conductive tape and then covered with RAM. Paint-type RAM was available, but it had to be built up by hand, coat by coat. Even the gaps around the canopy and the fuel-filler door had to be filled with paint-type RAM before each flight. Ground crews had to even make sure that all surface screws were completely tight, since even one loose screw for an access panel could make the aircraft show up like a "barn door coming over the horizon" during radar signature testing at Groom Lake.

The cockpit on HAVE BLUE was located fairly far aft, probably best from an RCS perspective. But a combat aircraft needs to make certain concessions to operational considerations, and the cockpit was moved further forward on the SENIOR TREND. (Lockheed Martin Skunk Works)

ing, Park severely injured his back on impact. The aircraft was written off, and Bill Park was forced to retire from flying as a result.

The second HAVE BLUE made its maiden flight on 20 July 1978 with Major Norman "Ken" Dyson at the controls. This aircraft did not have the flight test instrument boom or spin recovery parachute and was covered with RAM to minimize its radar signature. This aircraft also had nose wheel steering, something the first aircraft lacked.

HB1002 proved to be essentially undetectable by all airborne radars except the Boeing E-3 AWACS, which could only acquire the aircraft at short ranges. Most ground-based missile tracking radars could

detect the HAVE BLUE only after it was well inside the minimum range for the surface-to-air missiles with which they were associated. Neither ground-based radars nor air-to-air missile guidance radars could lock onto the aircraft. It was found that the best tactic to avoid radar detection was to approach the radar site head on, presenting the HAVE BLUE's small nose-on signature.

The application of the RAM was rather tricky, and ground crews had to be careful to seal all joints thoroughly before each flight. Originally the RAM came in linoleum-like sheets which were cut to shape and bonded to the skin to cover large areas. Doors and access panels had to be carefully adjusted to tight tolerances between flights

Originally the program had scheduled 55 flights for the second aircraft, but on 11 July 1979, during its 52nd test flight, the aircraft suffered a double hydraulic failure and fire. Major Dyson successfully ejected and was not injured, but the aircraft was a total loss. Since the project was winding down in any case, the loss of the aircraft had minimal impact. The wreckage of both HAVE BLUEs was subsequently buried somewhere on the Groom Lake reservation.

Some aspects of the aerodynamic portion of the HAVE BLUE test program have been released and are discussed in Jay Miller's *Skunk Works'* and in *HAVE BLUE and the F-117A* by Aronstein and Piccirillo. In contrast, very little has been released on the RCS evaluation of the HAVE BLUE demonstrators, although they were obviously fairly successful since the Air Force subsequently proceeded with a developed version of the basic configuration.

[1] David C. Aronstein and Albert C. Piccirillo, *HAVE BLUE and the F-117A – Evolution of the "Stealth Fighter"*, American Institute of Aeronautics and Astronautics, Reston, VA, 1997, p 14. [2] The Yehudi Lights evolved from theoretical studies and experiments during the 1930s, eventually culminating in flight tests using Grumman TBF and Consolidated B-24s during World War II. Additional tests were conducted during the late 1960s using McDonnell Douglas F-4 Phantom IIs sponsored by the COMPASS project office. [3] Jon Lake, *Lockheed Martin F-117 – Under the Skin of the Black Jet*, AIR International, August 1998. [4] Robert F. Door, *Lockheed F-117 Nighthawk*, World Air Power Journal Special, Aerospace Publishing, Ltd. 1995. [5] There have been reports that XST stood for "Experimental Stealth Testbed," but this is unlikely given the term stealth had not been widely used in relation to aircraft at the time, and would have been too much of a security compromise in any case. [6] Jay Miller, *Lockheed Martin's Skunk Works*, Midland Counties Publishing, 1995, p 161. [7] *Ibid*, p 161. [8] David C. Aronstein and Albert C. Piccirillo, *HAVE BLUE and the F-117A – Evolution of the "Stealth Fighter"*, American Institute of Aeronautics and Astronautics, Reston, VA, 1997, p 42.

SENIOR TREND

On 10 October 1977, DARPA awarded a contract to Lockheed to facilitate exploring possible production versions of the HAVE BLUE demonstrator. DARPA defined two possible configurations for Lockheed to investigate. The "A-Model" called for an Advanced Technology Aircraft (ATA) using the basic HAVE BLUE configuration with a 400-nm radius of action carrying a 5,000-pound payload. The F404-powered aircraft would be 64 feet long with a 43-foot wingspan and a gross takeoff weight of 43,000 pounds. The "B-Model" doubled both the radius of action and the payload. This version would be 76 feet long with a 47-foot wingspan and a gross takeoff weight of 90,000 pounds. Power would come from a pair of modified General Electric F101 engines from the B-1 program. Lockheed determined that the ATA-A could probably be built, but the ATA-B was unlikely given the current aerodynamic configuration of the HAVE BLUE design. DARPA subsequently relaxed the B-Model payload requirements to 7,500 pounds, but Lockheed still did not believe it could be built quickly or economically.[1]

In the end, DARPA passed the results of the concept exploration contract to the Air Force which decided that the ATA-A offered sufficient promise to issue a full-scale development contract to Lockheed on 16 November 1977 under the name SENIOR TREND. Although initially based on the HAVE BLUE configuration, SENIOR TREND rapidly diverged in several important ways. First, the wing sweep was reduced to solve some of the center-of-gravity problems experienced during wind tunnel (and subsequent flight testing) of the HAVE BLUE design. The forward fuselage was

A detailed mockup of the SENIOR TREND was built by Lockheed during late 1979 in Building 309/310 at Burbank. The aft-fuselage closeout is interesting in that it appears to angle upward, a feature that does not appear on the production aircraft. (Lockheed Martin Skunk Works)

A considerable amount of time on various test ranges has been accumulated by scale models of the SENIOR TREND. Much of this time has been to carefully measure the signature of the aircraft from different perspectives to allow a complete understanding of how the aircraft can be used in combat. This quarter-scale model is used at the Lockheed test facility at Helendale, California, not far from the Skunk Works' home at Palmdale. At various times the models have worn the tailcodes of each of the operational wings that have operated the Nighthawk. (Skunk Works/Denny Lombard)

WARBIRDTECH
SERIES

made shorter to allow the pilot and planned sensors to have a better view over the nose. The Platypus body flap was deleted, and both inboard and outboard elevons were fitted to the training edge of the wing. However, the most visible change was the vertical stabilizers – they now canted outboard from the centerline instead of canting inboard from the outer parts of the body. The change to the vertical stabilizers had been proposed by Skunk Works as early as February 1978, just three months after the first HAVE BLUE flight. Although creating a slightly larger RCS signature, they offered far better stability.

SENIOR TREND also spent a considerable amount of time in various wind tunnels, with Lockheed engineers trying to understand if the aircraft would actually fly. Very few concessions were made to aerodynamics in the final design. (Lockheed Martin)

A great deal of computer time with the ECHO program was necessary to design the SENIOR TREND, and a 60%-scale model was tested at the RATSCAT range during April 1979 to get some real-world measurements on the design as it evolved. It was recognized from the beginning that SENIOR TREND would not achieve better results than HAVE BLUE. In fact, the primary goal was to achieve a similar RCS with a militarily useful aircraft.[2]

Interestingly, SENIOR TREND was only one of five stealth programs being managed by the Classified Aeronautical Systems Program Office at Wright-Patterson AFB. The others were the Advanced Technol-ogy Bomber (later to become the B-2), the Tri-Service Standoff Attack Missile (TASSM – later cancelled and replaced by JASSM), Northrop's TACIT BLUE program, and the Low Observables Technology Base, which collected stealth data for use by the other programs.

Unlike the HAVE BLUE designs, which had carried minimal equipment, the SENIOR TREND was intended from the beginning to be an operational attack aircraft. Provisions were made for a pair of weapons bays under the fuselage and for various sensors in the nose. Each of the weapons bays was sized to accommodate a single 2,000-pound laser-guided bomb (LGB), although other weapons could be accommodated, including a B61 tactical nuclear weapon.

The nose would house a pair of forward-looking infrared (FLIR) sensors coupled with laser designators, one above and one below the nose. But these presented some interesting design challenges – the major being how to make the sensors invisible to radar. The initial thought was to hide the sensors behind panels made from gallium arsenide or zinc selenide glass, but this proved too expensive (estimates ranged as high as $500,000 per installation). Some experiments were made trying to develop perforated panels that would block radar yet allow the passage of laser energy, but none were found that could withstand the acoustic and air loads encountered in flight. The eventual solution was to use a fine copper mesh screen that presented a solid facet to microwave energy yet was transparent to laser radiation. The mesh was sufficiently strong to withstand the air loads encountered at high subsonic speeds.

A great deal had to be explored on the way to determining the control laws necessary for the SENIOR TREND's flight computers. To assist in understanding these laws, Lockheed used a very old aircraft. The Calspan NT-33A had begun life as a two-seat P-80, and was later modified with an F-94A nose. When Calspan (Cornell Aero Laboratory)

acquired it, they modified it into a variable-stability trainer – a role it would perform until the 1990s when it was finally replaced by the VISTA F-16. Although the NT-33 was capable of simulating varied responses to a pilot's input, it was not capable of simulating the dynamically unstable SENIOR TREND aerodynamic configuration. Nevertheless, it served a useful purpose in allowing Lockheed to check some control law theories prior to the SENIOR TREND's first flight.

SENIOR TREND was a black project, and Lockheed went to considerable lengths to make sure it stayed that way. One of the easiest ways to determine that a new product is being developed by a manufacturer is to watch his suppliers. Components such as engines, flight control computers, large forgings for the landing gear, and various electronic components are normally supplied by outside manufacturers.

In an effort to eliminate this potential security leak, and also to save time and money, Lockheed elected to use as many already available components as possible. The engine would be a non-afterburning version of the General Electric F404 used by the F/A-18. The heads-up display (HUD), ejection seat, control column, and minor cockpit furnishings would also come from the F/A-18. The flight control computers would again come from the F-16 program, while the landing gear would come from the F-15. The inertial navigation system would come from stocks maintained for the B-52. The FLIR equipment would also be off-the-shelf, coming from some of the more interesting OV-10D derivatives (and also used on some P-3 aircraft).[3]

It was possible for Lockheed and the Air Force to simply procure these parts from available inventory, or to order more as spare parts, and nobody was the wiser. Combined with a relatively small and dedicated workforce, this helped ensure the SENIOR TREND would remain a secret.

There were challenges remaining for the design team. The flush air data ports on the HAVE BLUE aircraft had almost worked, but they were clearly unacceptable for an operational aircraft. After examining every idea they could conceive of, Lockheed engineers finally decided there was no alternative except to use conventional pitot-static tubes. The only acceptable location for the tubes was on the

A full-scale SENIOR TREND was also tested on an RCS measurement range. Most of the testing was conducted at night to minimize the chances of the aircraft being seen by uncleared personnel and passing satellites. (Lockheed Martin Skunk Works)

Despite its rather bizarre appearance, the SENIOR TREND was of completely conventional construction. Since the aircraft was not meant to fly supersonically, aluminum was used extensively. (Lockheed Martin Skunk Works)

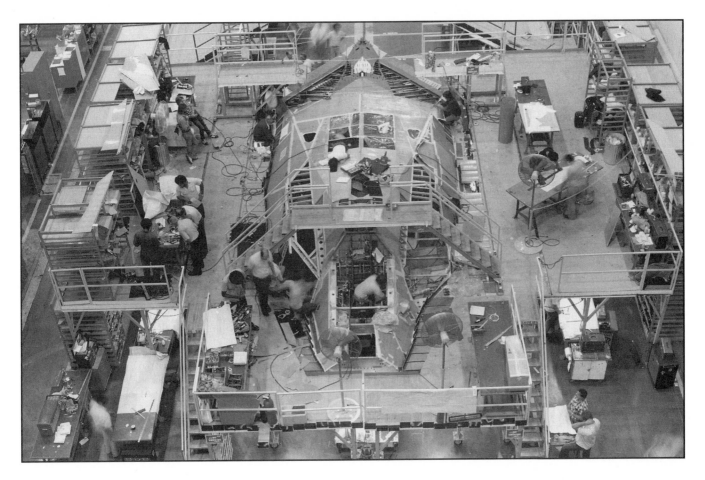

The large intakes are clearly visible in the photo below before the final structure is installed. The overall size of the airframe may be compared to the men around and in it. (Lockheed Martin Skunk Works)

leading edge of the wing just ahead of the cockpit. In an attempt to reduce the signature of the ports as much as possible, the ports use a faceted shape. It took a lot of experimentation to provide probes that had orifices sufficiently large to gather acceptable air data, yet small enough to have minimal impact on the RCS.

The initial order was for five Full-Scale Development (FSD) aircraft, although the Tactical Air Command (TAC) quickly established a requirement for 20 production versions. Two of the FSD aircraft would be refurbished, allowing TAC a single 18 aircraft squadron and four attrition aircraft. This squadron was envisioned as a "silver bullet" unit capable of conducting covert operations under the concept of "plausible deniability." A secret base was ordered built at Tonopah, Nevada, to conceal SENIOR TREND.[4]

By 1981, there was pressure from within TAC to increase the number of SENIOR TREND aircraft substantially in order to equip a larger "black" unit at Tonopah, and a more

visible unit at a second location, most probably Holloman AFB, New Mexico. Although Lockheed was keeping the project within budget (a Skunk Works tradition), the necessary funding could not be found, and in the end only 59 aircraft were ordered. These were assigned to a single Wing at Tonopah with two squadrons of 18 aircraft each, nine training aircraft, four spares, and ten attrition aircraft.

An incident early in the test program at Groom Lake gave the SENIOR TREND two of its nicknames. A Baja Scorpion found its way into one of the buildings and onto an engineer's desk. Since the scorpion was not wearing a badge, and apparently had no security clearance to be in the area, it was unceremoniously eliminated. A drawing of a scorpion subsequently appeared on the first SENIOR TREND aircraft and in some Lockheed literature. Having survived the scorpion incident without harm, some pilots and maintenance personnel began to refer to the usually deadly insect as a "cockroach," a name some also applied to the air-

craft themselves. Both of these names have been used internally to the program for years.

First Flight

When the SENIOR TREND program had begun, it was expected that the first aircraft would fly in July 1980. But Lockheed ran into some difficulties in assembling the aircraft, and the program ran about a year behind schedule. Many of these difficulties were directly related to the "stealth" properties of many parts – for instance a certain ferrite paint Lockheed was using suddenly lost its radar-absorbent properties. The cause was a slight, and seemingly harmless, change to the manufacturing process. Problems were compounded by the fact that suppliers did not know what their parts were being used for (it was a black program, after all), and many of the suppliers did not even know Lockheed was their customer (the parts being procured through a variety of middlemen and dummy companies). Probably the most serious problems were with developing the complex tailpipe,

The first SENIOR TREND after being painted overall light grey. Note the perforated grill over the FLIR sensor, later replaced by a mesh screen. The early five pitot probes are visible on the nose – later one was deleted, accounting for the current configuration. (Lockheed Martin Skunk Works)

One of the FSD SENIOR TREND's during an early test flight. The names on the canopy sill were those of test pilots Hal Farley, Skip Anderson, and Dave Ferguson. Note the configuration of the exhaust ducts – the upper surfaces terminate well before the lower surface, hiding most of the IR signature from ground-based observer. The five pitot tubes show up well from this angle. (U.S. Air Force via Lockheed Martin Skunk Works)

which ran into difficulties that would not be fully solved until well after production ended.

In May 1981, the first SENIOR TREND (Lockheed number 780) was finally shipped to Groom Lake inside a Lockheed C-5A Galaxy, much like the HAVE BLUEs before it. Fuel leaks were encountered during subsequent ground testing, delaying the first flight by several weeks. Finally, on 18 June 1981, Harold "Hal" Farley, Jr. took the first SENIOR TREND on its maiden flight.

During initial flight testing it was noted that directional stability was less than ideal, and after the tenth flight the aircraft was modified with larger vertical stabilizers in an attempt to correct this. The second aircraft made its maiden flight on 24 September 1981, also with the small verticals, but received the larger units after its fourth flight.

There has been a great deal of controversy over the serial numbers of the SENIOR TREND aircraft. The first aircraft was simply called "780," seemingly a reference to its originally planned first flight date. Subsequent aircraft were sequentially numbered through 844. However, it appears that bureaucracy got the better of the program after it emerged from the black world, and the sequential numbers were converted to serial numbers (by simply assigning a fiscal year prefix to them) after the fact. Most Air force documentation now lists them as standard "FY-xxxx" serial numbers beginning with 79-1780, and this is what is currently seen painted on the tail of each aircraft. Interestingly, the new serial numbers span five fiscal years, but the last three digits remain in sequence, an unlikely occurrence. On most aircraft, the number has been incremented by 1,000 to avoid conflicts with other serial numbers assigned to those years.

As in most flight test programs, each of the FSD aircraft (they were technically not prototypes) was assigned a specific mission. The first aircraft (780) was used primarily for aerodynamic testing, including loads, flutter, and high angle-of-attack investigations. It was also used to open the in-flight refueling envelope. This aircraft was outwardly different from subsequent aircraft in the use of five pitot-static probes instead of four. Between December 1983 and February 1984, a set of extended wing leading edges was fitted as a way to reduce landing speeds. The tests appear to have been successful, reducing landing speed by about 10 knots, but production aircraft did not incorporate the change. Eventually the first aircraft was retired, and now sits on a pole at Nellis AFB.

The second aircraft (781) also flew with five probes for its first four flights, but was converted to the production configuration at the same time its vertical stabilizers were changed. It also received provisions for the sensor suite at the same time, although it is unclear if it was ever fitted with the sensors themselves. The aircraft was used for icing tests, weapons release trials, and acoustic (panel flutter) evaluations. On 18 December 1981, the aircraft was again grounded for modifications, this time to receive the RAM coating and various tweaks to panel lines to reduce the RCS. The aircraft flew the first SENIOR TREND RCS measurement mission on 23 January 1982. At the conclusion of the test program, this aircraft was donated to the Air Force Museum.

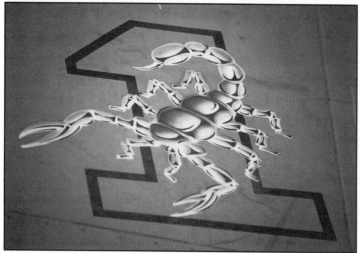

Only Anderson's and Farley's names appeared on the canopy frame when this photograph was taken. The scorpion emblem superimposed over the 1 was only applied to the first aircraft (780). The faceted plates were not installed on several of the FSD aircraft during the test program since they were not being used for RCS measurements. Note that even the small plates covering the canopy release and emergency jettison switches are faceted. The screen over the air intake does not disrupt airflow as much as would be expected, and presents a reasonably even pressure distribution at the compressor face. (Skunk Works/Denny Lombard and Eric Schulzinger)

Hal Farley stands in front of the first SENIOR TREND after its first flight on 18 June 1981. Although difficult to discern in this photo, the aircraft is painted in the three-tone disruptive camouflage. (Lockheed Martin Skunk Works)

The third FSD aircraft (782) got off to a rough start on 18 December 1981 when it aborted its first flight because of high engine exhaust temperatures. The aircraft was used primarily for weapons release testing, weapons integration, avionics development, and it also participated in the Initial Operational Test and Evaluation (IOT&E) trials. This aircraft is currently assigned to the test squadron at Palmdale.

The primary RCS and signature test vehicle was the fourth aircraft (783), which made its first flight on 7 July 1982. This was a good deal later than expected, the delay a result of difficulties achieving a uniform RAM coating over the entire aircraft. This was the only FSD aircraft to feature the production canopy configuration with a variety of facets at its leading edge and along the side glass. This aircraft is currently assigned to the test squadron at Palmdale.

The last FSD aircraft (784) made its first flight on 10 April 1982 and was used primarily for avionics and navigation system development. This aircraft is also currently assigned to the test squadron at Palmdale.

Initially the first FSD aircraft was painted in a disruptive camouflage of blue, gray, and sand in an attempt to hide its multi-faceted design. As with the HAVE BLUE, this proved somewhat ineffective, and the aircraft was repainted an overall light gray after a few months. The rest of the FSD aircraft were painted light gray from the beginning. Eventually the Air Force decided that all future aircraft would be painted black, and the FSD aircraft were later similarly repainted.

The first production SENIOR TREND (785) made its only flight on 20 April 1982. In an error that would be repeated again during

Late in the test program, the Air Force directed that the SENIOR TRENDs would be painted black instead of the light grey used by the five FSD aircraft. The exhaust "slot" shows up well here, including the vanes used to redirect the exhaust directly to the rear instead of angling off to the side. (Skunk Works/Eric Schulzinger)

SENIOR TREND, the aircraft's alpha and yaw sensors were wired backwards, confusing the stability control system, and causing the aircraft to crash during takeoff. Lockheed test pilot Robert L. Riedenauer was seriously injured and retired from flying. Since the aircraft had not completed its acceptance flight, the Air Force did not pay for the aircraft, leaving Lockheed to foot the bill. The remains of the aircraft were later combined with parts from the fatigue test airframe (number 777) to construct a display aircraft that currently sits outside the Skunk Works in Palmdale. It should be noted that a structural test airframe (779) was also constructed.[5] Although conclusive documentation could not be found, airframe number 778 was most likely assigned to the engineering mockup.

Initial Operating Capability

The first SENIOR TREND to be turned over to the Air Force was 787, which was handed over on 23 August 1982. The aircraft was used by the Combined Test Force to support continued IOT&E. The first aircraft to be delivered to a combat unit was 786, assigned to the 4450th Test Group on 2 September 1982.[6]

The 4450th TG had been formed on 15 October 1979 specifically to operate the SENIOR TREND. The "Group" designation was intended to attract less attention than a "Wing," and the cover story was that the Group was conducting operations and tactics evaluations using LTV A-7D/K Corsair IIs. The Group would eventually have four assigned squadrons: 4450th Test Squadron ("Nightstalkers"), 4451st TS ("Ghostriders"), 4452nd TS ("Goat Suckers"), and the 4453rd Test and Evaluation Squadron (TES – "Grim Reapers").

By the time the first SENIOR TREND was delivered, the Group had 20 A-7s and three Mitsubishi MU-2 business aircraft on strength. The MU-2s were used to shuttle personnel between Nellis, Groom Lake, Tonopah, and Burbank. A chartered Boeing 727 was also used to transport personnel between Nellis and Tonopah. The A-7s, in addition to providing a convenient cover story, provided

proficiency training to the pilots assigned to the group. When the Air Force retired the A-7 fleet, several T-38s were brought in to fill this role.

By 1982 it was obvious that the SENIOR TREND aircraft would have to move out of Groom Lake when they became operational.[7] Although Groom Lake is the ideal location for a secret test program, and has been used effectively for that purpose for many years, it did not have the facilities to house a complete operational unit. Nor did it want to. When limited to a few pilots and maintenance technicians that had all been very rigorously screened, security could be maintained, and although not desirable,

it probably did not matter much if one group got a glimpse of some other project. But the numbers of personnel required to support an operational unit would severely compromise the security of other on-going programs.

A location on the Tonopah Test Range was selected to build a secret airfield for the SENIOR TREND program. Although there had been bases at Tonopah since World War II, none were in the particular location selected for the stealth fighters. The base was completed in record time, and by early 1983 some SENIOR TREND operations had moved to the new base. The airfield was located 32 miles southeast of Tonopah, Nevada,

which itself is about 140 miles northwest of Las Vegas. The Tonopah airfield was new, and it was well guarded. Double rows of fencing, each topped with barbed wire, encircled the entire base. The latest techniques for reading palm-prints were incorporated at the gates to the flight line, ensuring only those people with the correct clearances could gain entry. Individual hangers were built for each of the SENIOR TREND aircraft, much like had been done for the A-12s and SR-71s before them. The aircraft were never outdoors except when taxing to or from the runway. Except for some security forces, nobody lived at or near the Tonopah base – all SENIOR TREND personnel were

The "secret" base at Tonopah that was built specifically for the SENIOR TREND program. Unlike most Air Force bases, Tonopah did not include housing and other social infrastructure. Except for some security personnel, everybody lived at Nellis AFB, near Las Vegas. (Lockheed Martin Skunk Works)

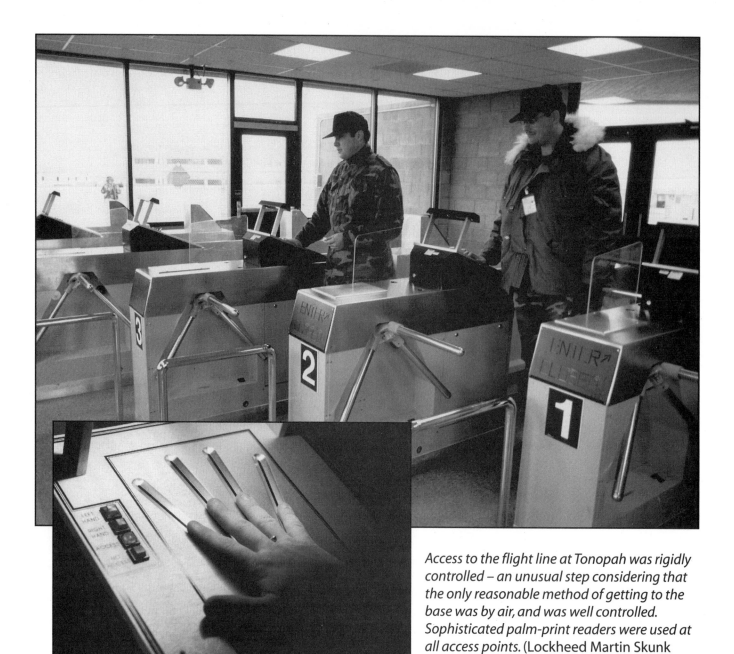

Access to the flight line at Tonopah was rigidly controlled – an unusual step considering that the only reasonable method of getting to the base was by air, and was well controlled. Sophisticated palm-print readers were used at all access points. (Lockheed Martin Skunk Works)

housed at Nellis and commuted in the 727 or MU-2s.

The 4450th TG achieved a limited IOC at Tonopah on 28 October 1983 when the tenth SENIOR TREND arrived. Eight of the aircraft were, in theory, able to be deployed within 48 hours of notification, and eight pilots had passed all the training necessary to be considered combat-ready. The other two aircraft could be deployed in 72 hours, although their pilots had not been through all required training.

But things were not going as well as hoped. Continued problems with tailpipe overheating limited both the performance of the SENIOR TREND, as well as significantly increasing the maintenance effort required to keep the aircraft flying.[8]

Weapons testing was not progressing as rapidly as planned either, and at the end of 1983 only the GBU-10 and Mk 84 had been cleared for the aircraft (as well as the BDU-33 practice bomb). Work was continuing on clearing the SUU-30 and B61, and evaluations were being made as to what other weapons would fit with the tactics being developed by the 4450th. The flight envelope was also not being opened as fast as planned, primarily because of concerns over the tailpipes and vertical

Most personnel traveled to Tonopah from Nellis in a chartered 727 that ran a scheduled service between the two locations. Several MU-2 business turboprops were also used. The sign on the terminal in the background was not sincere – visitors were not particularly welcome. (Lockheed Martin Skunk Works)

stabilizers. Although originally intended to operate within the old[9] Air Force fighter limitations (+7.33/-3g, and 14 units AoA), this had been reduced[10] to +6/-3g to avoid structural weight growth, and at the end of 1983 the aircraft was only cleared for +4/-1g and 10 units AoA. In addition, maximum speed was limited to Mach 0.8 instead of the intended Mach 0.9.

SENIOR TREND was also supposed to use a sophisticated automated mission planning system that was also running into development trouble. Fortunately, the lack of this system only meant missions had to be planned by hand – a task that took 8-10 hours per mission.

No real simulator existed for pilot training during the first few years of the program. Instead, pilots

The F-15 heritage of the undercarriage is obvious, although only the major castings and actuators are identical. (Skunk Works/Denny Lombard and Eric Schulzinger)

trained in an old-fashioned no-motion procedural trainer at Burbank. Eventually a six-axis-of-freedom visual dynamic simulator was developed and installed at Tonopah. There was also no two-seat conversion trainer for the SENIOR TREND. There had been discussions about using the damaged first-production airframe as the basis for a two-seat trainer (much as had been done for the OXCART A-12), but nothing ever came of it.

All of the SENIOR TREND aircraft were manufactured at Burbank and transported to either Groom Lake or Tonopah in C-5s where they were reassembled and made their first flights. No first flights were made from Burbank. In transit the aircraft was covered with tarps supported by rectangular frames to hide the aircraft's unusual shape.[11]

The F-117A's radar signature has been reported as between 0.1 and 0.01 square meters. By comparison, an F-4 had a front RCS of over 6 square meters. In theory this allows the F-117A to get 90% closer to a given radar without being detected than was possible with the F-4.

A SENIOR TREND is prepared for a training mission from Tonopah. Note the lights along the side of the fuselage that allow the pilot to examine the air intakes for ice. Like the F-16, the canopy also includes the forward wind screen, although unlike the F-16 the visibility is blocked by heavy framing around the transparencies. The faceting of the forward fuselage shows up well in this photo. (Skunk Works/Denny Lombard and Eric Schulzinger)

[1] Lockheed Report SP4763F, *Advanced Technology Aircraft (ATA) Budget and Schedule Summary*, 27 February 1978. [2] David C. Aronstein and Albert C. Piccirillo, *HAVE BLUE and the F-117A – Evolution of the "Stealth Fighter"*, American Institute of Aeronautics and Astronautics, Reston, VA, 1997, p 61. [3] Jay Miller, *Lockheed Martin's Skunk Works*, Midland Counties Publishing, 1995, p 165. [4] Jon Lake, *Lockheed Martin F-117 – Under the Skin of the Black Jet*, AIR International, August 1998. [5] David C. Aronstein and Albert C. Piccirillo, *HAVE BLUE and the F-117A – Evolution of the "Stealth Fighter"*, American Institute of Aeronautics and Astronautics, Reston, VA, 1997, p 75. [6] Jon Lake, *Lockheed Martin F-117 – Under the Skin of the Black Jet*, AIR International, August 1998. [7] Robert F. Dorr, *Lockheed F-117 Nighthawk*, World Air Power Journal Special, 1995, p 22. [8] David C. Aronstein and Albert C. Piccirillo, *HAVE BLUE and the F-117A – Evolution of the "Stealth Fighter"*, American Institute of Aeronautics and Astronautics, Reston, VA, 1997, p 138. [9] Beginning with the McDonnell Douglas F-15 Eagle, these standards were raised to +9/-5g and unlimited AoA. [10] David C. Aronstein and Albert C. Piccirillo, *HAVE BLUE and the F-117A – Evolution of the "Stealth Fighter"*, American Institute of Aeronautics and Astronautics, Reston, VA, 1997, p 158. [11] Robert F. Dorr, *Lockheed F-117 Nighthawk*, World Air Power Journal Special, 1995, p 18.

SENIOR TREND number 802 during a semi-stealth mode flight. The aircraft's antennas and navigation lights are deployed, but no radar reflectors are fitted. The markings on the forward fuselage have changed over time – here only an ejection seat warning triangle is shown, but at other times the normal "emergency instruction" blocks and arrows have also been applied. (Skunk Works/Eric Schulzinger)

Security between the runway and flight line at Tonopah was also tight. Notice the double row of fencing. Also notice the temporary guard shack – apparently the airfield designers had forgotten to build a permanent structure. This is one of the Northrop T-38 Talons used by Tonopah after the A-7s were retired. The T-38s were painted a very attractive three-tone gloss grey with "TR" tailcodes. (Skunk Works/Denny Lombard and Eric Schulzinger)

The ground intercom connection is inside the front wheel well. Here a Lockheed crew performs a final check of a SENIOR TREND at Palmdale before a test flight. (Skunk Works/Eric Schulzinger)

The SENIOR TREND was equipped with a braking parachute, which proved especially useful in the early years since the standard F-15 brakes were barely adequate to stop the aircraft due to its high landing speeds. When the carbon-carbon brakes for the F-15E were introduced this became less of a problem. The braking chutes have come in a variety of colors including white, black, and green. (Craig Kaston via Mick Roth Collection)

An early refueling test using a KC-135. Note the long pitot probe on the closest SENIOR TREND, which also appears to be painted gray instead of black. One of the 4450th's A-7Ds is in the background observing the test. The Nighthawk has relatively short legs, and has to rely on in-flight refueling for most missions. (U.S. Air Force)

The hangers at Tonopah were modern and well equipped, having been built specifically to house SENIOR TREND. Note the lowered trapeze in the weapons bay and the 37th FW tail markings on this aircraft. (Skunk Works/Denny Lombard and Eric Schulzinger)

The primary weapon used by the Nighthawk is the laser guided bomb, seen here in a test drop from SENIOR TREND 784. Note the two camera pods under the wings to photograph the drop. This aircraft appears to have more antennas on the upper fuselage and under the nose than operational aircraft. (U.S. Air Force)

SENIOR TREND 832 at Tonopah. Note the aircraft number on the nose gear strut. Also notice the taxi/landing lights on each main gear strut – a change from the F-15. Another light is on the nose gear strut next to the landing gear door (partially obscured in this photo). (Skunk Works/Denny Lombard and Eric Schulzinger)

Aircraft 800 preparing to takeoff from Holloman on 23 September 1996. THe main landing gear doors are always opened on the ground prior to takeoff, even if the aircraft had taxied with them closed. (Charles E. Stewart via Mick Roth Collection

SENIOR TREND is an odd looking aircraft from any angle, including head on. The bottom of the aircraft is almost flat, unlike the HAVE BLUE demonstrators that had a pronounced "V" shape. Reportedly this resulted in the SENIOR TREND being easier to locate by radar when painted from the bottom, although normal tactics call for low-level flight, minimizing this exposure. (Skunk Works/Denny Lombard and Eric Schulzinger)

OUT OF THE BLACK

There has been a lot of speculation about how and when the F-117A designation was applied to the SENIOR TREND program. As a designation it makes little sense given what has been publicly acknowledged by the Air Force, especially since there apparently was no F-112 through F-116. There is no real point speculating over where the designation came from, but sometime in the mid 1980s, as SENIOR TREND began to emerge from its black world, the aircraft became known as F-117As.

The aircraft's shortcomings at IOC convinced the Air Force to release some funding for upgrades to bring the aircraft up to its original expectations. Primarily the first modifications were aimed at improving the aircraft's weapons carrying capabilities. The Offensive Capability Improvement Program (OCIP) consisted of three distinct phases. The $191 million OCIP I replaced the aircraft's original three Delco M362F mission computers with three Mil-Std-1750A-compliant IBM AP-102 computers communicating over dual-redundant Mil-Std-1553B data busses. The OCIP I was also known as the Weapons Systems Computational Subsystem (WSCS) upgrade. The AP-101/102 series of computers has been used in everything from the B-52 and B-1, to the Space Shuttle. The adaptation of a Mil-Std-1750A-compliant computer (and its associated data busses) allowed the integration of new Air Force "smart" precision-guided weapons without a lengthy development cycle.

The first offensive weapon to take advantage of this on the F-117A was the GBU-27 Paveway III laser-guided bomb. The Paveway III system was a tremendous improvement over the earlier laser-guided bombs. Previous weapons had "zigzagged" their way to a target because their flight controls could only be positioned full-up, full-down, or neutral. This tended to limit their accuracy since the in-flight corrections were rather crude. It also resulted in a poor impact angle which limited the penetration of the weapon.[1]

Paveway III added full-authority flight controls that allowed the bombs to fly much more stable trajectories to their targets. Since corrections could be made quicker

The facets on the leading edge of the canopy look like they would present an interesting obstacle to entering the cockpit. Note the slight indentation on the forward part of the nose gear door to clear the nose wheel. (Skunk Works/Denny Lombard)

The OCIP II modifications included the ability to open both weapons bay doors at the same time to allow a near-simultaneous drop of both laser guided bombs. Note the tail fins of the upper bomb have not opened yet, while the ones on the lower bomb are fully deployed. (Lockheed Martin Skunk Works)

and more accurately, the bombs could also attack targets from a much steeper trajectory, allowing the weapon to penetrate further.

Unfortunately, the Paveway III capability proved to be much more difficult to add to the F-117A than had been anticipated. The original Paveway III was the GBU-24 and, much like the SENIOR TREND, it had been developed in considerable secrecy. As a result, the F-117A's weapons bays were too small to accommodate the weapon; the tail fins were too large and the guidance section adapter was too long. Air Force and Lockheed personnel quickly devised a GBU-XX that used the new Paveway III guidance section attached to a Mk 84 2,000 pound

bomb equipped with the older (and smaller) Paveway II tail unit. Although this traded away some of the improved accuracy of the Paveway III, it was small enough to fit inside the F-117A weapon bays. A production version of the GBU-XX was subsequently ordered under the GBU-27 designation.

Originally, only one of the two weapons doors could be opened at once. OCIP I added new composite doors that removed this restriction, and both weapons bays may now be opened simultaneously. The first F-117A equipped with the OCIP I modifications was redelivered to the Air Force in November 1987, and all F-117As had been modified by June 1992.[2]

The second phase of the OCIP upgrade addressed some concerns pilots had expressed about the cockpit equipment. As delivered from Lockheed, the F-117A had used Texas Instruments monochrome displays for most flight instrumentation, and a monochrome CRT to display the FLIR imagery. The TI displays were replaced with new Honeywell color multi-function displays (from late model F/A-18s) that could display flight instrumentation and FLIR data. This freed up room in the instrument panel for a new Harris digital moving map display to provide better navigational data.

OCIP II also added a Pilot Activated Automatic Recovery System

As on most Air Force fighters, the refueling receptacle on the F-117A is located on the centerline of the aircraft behind the cockpit where the pilot cannot see it. Reportedly the Nighthawk does not exhibit any unusual characteristics during in-flight refueling, and the aircraft is cleared to refuel from both KC-135 and KC-10 tankers. (Lockheed Martin/Judson Brohmer)

(PAARS). This is similar to a system installed in many Russian aircraft that commands the flight control system to return the aircraft to a known straight-and-level attitude, and is particularly useful if a pilot becomes disoriented during night missions. In the F-117A's case the system is activated at the press of a button on the throttle.

The improved mission computers added during OCIP I allowed the incorporation of a Flight Management System during the second phase. This system couples the autopilot and autothrottle functions to allow the computers to fly the aircraft to a predesignated geographic position, at a specified altitude, within ±1 second of the desired time. Given the nature of most F-117A tactics, which demand highly coordinated attacks at various locations simultaneously, this greatly improves the pilot's ability to perform his mission.

The OCIP II conversions began with aircraft 805, which made its first flight on 1 December 1988, and redeliveries began two years later. All aircraft had been modified by the end of 1993.

OCIP III was aimed at replacing some avionics that had become obsolete and were no longer supported in the maintenance channels. The original Honeywell SPN-GEANS inertial guidance system (INS) was replaced with a Honeywell H-423/E ring-laser gyro. This change greatly reduced the pre-mission setup necessary for the F-117A. The original INS had required up to 45 minutes to align at a precisely known location on the airfield, and had a mean-time-between-failures (MTBF) of only 400 hours. The new laser-ring INS requires only five minutes to align and has an MTBF of over 2,000 hours. Interestingly, the older unit was slightly more accurate.

During Desert Storm the usefulness of the Global Positioning System (GPS) became fully understood, and like many Air Force aircraft a GPS receiver was subsequently ordered installed on the F-117A. The GPS receiver is tied into the INS, and has greatly improved

All three landing gear retract forward without any other manipulation. The nose gear is covered by a single door, while the main gear are covered by two-piece doors. One piece is fixed to the gear strut, while the other can be closed while the aircraft is on the ground. (Skunk Works/Denny Lombard and Eric Schulzinger)

An F-117A (816) from the 7th FS at Holloman over White Sands, New Mexico. (Lockheed Martin/Tom Reynolds)

the accuracy of the aircraft's navigational systems. A stealthy GPS antenna had been developed as part of the ATF (F-22) program, and is being used on the F-117A. Total cost of the GPS upgrade was $101 million, and is expected to be completed in October 1999.[3]

The engine exhausts continued to present problems for the F-117A during the first ten years of its service life despite repeated modifications. New heat shields and thermal protection "bricks" (which line the inside of the ducts themselves) have been installed, and the entire duct has gone through several minor redesigns. This appears to be helping and the ducts are not reported to be particularly troublesome any longer.

Since the F-117A uses subsystems from a variety of aircraft, it tends to receive the same upgrades developed for those aircraft. For instance, when new carbon-carbon brakes were developed for the F-15E, the same brakes found their way onto the F-117A, finally eliminating some braking problems.

In July 1989, a new graphite thermoplastic vertical stabilizer was first flown. This was a response to several near-failures and one in-flight failure of the original units. The new vertical stabilizers were installed on the last few aircraft on the production line, and all other aircraft were retrofitted with it beginning in June 1990. Lockheed delivered the last new vertical stabilizer in June 1992, but all aircraft

were not modified until August 1994 when the last few F-117As rotated back to the U.S. from Saudi Arabia. The new units have allowed the F-117A's flight envelope to be opened closer to the original specifications.[4]

Even the exotic RAM has received some upgrades, mainly thanks to newer products developed for other programs such as the B-2 and F-22. The original RAM added almost 2,000 pounds to the empty weight of the aircraft. The new RAM, in addition to being slightly more effective, has reduced this to approximately 400 pounds. Lockheed subsequently developed a spray-on RAM that is much less maintenance intensive and somewhat more effective. There was a

An F-117A and KC-10 tanker bank while conducting refueling tests. There were minor concerns about the effect of the wake turbulence from the large KC-10 on the F-117, but flight tests revealed no unusual problems. (U.S. Air Force via Lockheed Martin)

great deal of difficulty getting the spray-on RAM to obtain a uniform thickness, but improved processes and materials have overcome these problems.[5] New electrochromic and thermalchromic coatings were also introduced, further reducing the aircraft's IR signature in certain wavelengths.

The original FLIR sensors were replaced after Desert Storm with improved Texas Instruments thermal imaging sensors. These have a greater range, are somewhat less sensitive to weather, and have a greater MTBF. The total cost of the upgrade was $144 million.[6] New radios, particularly low-probability-of-intercept (LPI) units, have

been added to allow pilots to communicate with theater commanders during missions.

Originally the F-117A went into combat observing complete radio silence to ensure the enemy could not locate the aircraft by tracking its emissions. But in late 1998, flight testing began on the "Integrated Real-time Information into the Cockpit/Real-time Information Out of the Cockpit for Combat Aircraft (IRRCA)" system for the F-117A. This is a secure high-bandwidth data link between either a high-flying U-2 or a satellite and the F-117A. The system uses an upward pointed LPI antenna and burst transmission, frequency-hopping, techniques that

are virtually impossible to trace from the ground (although it is possible an AWACS type aircraft might detect them momentarily). Incoming data from the link is displayed on the color moving map display, and can include status reports, updated target imagery, new navigational or targeting data, etc.

Data from the IRRCA can be fed directly to the Flight Management System which can replan the flight path in real time. The system then gives the pilot the option of accepting or rejecting the revised routing based on threat exposure, flight time, and fuel reserves. Updated threat data can also be downloaded in real-time to the FMS. The IRRCA

was first used during Operation Allied Force over Yugoslavia.

On 5 October 1989, the 37th Tactical Fighter Wing (TFW) took over the identity of the 4450th TG, but the unit remained at Tonopah. The 4450th TS became the 415th TFS, the 4451st TS became the 416th TFS, the 4453rd TES became the 417th Tactical Fighter Training Squadron (TFTS), and the 4452nd TS ceased to exist. In late 1992, the 415th TFS changed its name from "Nightstalkers" to "Nighthawks" as part of a general political correctness campaign in the Air Force, which also forced the 416th to change from "Ghostriders" to "Knight Riders." (The campaign in addition to trying to remove gender-specific and rude names, also removed all satanic ones).

Advanced Derivatives

Like most aircraft, many advanced derivatives of the F-117A have been proposed by the manufacturer and others. The first known variant was the F-117B (logically enough) that was first proposed in the early 1980s. This version featured an improved navigational capability (GPS, etc.), an LPI radar, and AGM-88A HARM missiles. This would allow the aircraft to conduct covert Wild Weasel missions plus improve its ability to hit targets of opportunity. An LPI radar antenna (basically a slightly modified B-1B unit) was reportedly[7] tested on an F-117A (784) during 1985, but this was more likely in support of the F-22 program. Nothing came of this proposal.

The F-117B designation was reused to describe a much more modified aircraft. In this proposal the wing sweep was reduced, wing span extended, and weapons bays significantly enlarged to allow a greater variety of weapons to be carried. The vertical stabilizers were reduced in both sweep and incline, and a conventional horizontal stabilizer was added. F414 engines developed for the still-borne Navy A-12 program were used, allowing an increase in gross takeoff weight to 73,250 pounds. Payload doubled to 8,000 pounds, while the radius of action increased to 1,000 nm. All of this would probably have had a detrimental effect on the stealth characteristics of the design, although no quantitative data could be ascertained.

Each hangar at Holloman can hold two F-117As (numbers can be seen above the doors). This aircraft is fitted with the radar reflectors on the fuselage just behind the stars and bars insignia. Also notice the open auxiliary doors on top of the intakes. (Skunk Works/Denny Lombard)

One of the advanced F-117 designs proposed for the U.S. Navy. Note the bubble canopy. The wing sweep is significantly reduced over the production F-117A, and a new conventional horizontal stabilizer has been added. There were always concerns over how well the delicate RAM would hold up under conditions at sea, and despite Lockheed's best marketing efforts, the Navy never seriously pursued an F-117 derivative. A similar aircraft was also marketed to the British Royal Air Force. (Lockheed Martin Skunk Works)

The U.S. Navy examined the F-117A in late 1984 with an eye towards acquiring a small contingent of the aircraft. As with all attempts to convert Air Force aircraft to meet Navy requirements, the F-117A did not fair well. A significant amount of structure would need to be strengthened to meets the rigors of catapult launches and arrested landings. This would significantly decrease the already marginal performance of the F-117A, especially before the new vertical stabilizers and exhaust ducts were installed. The effect of salt spray on the RAM was not fully understood, and the abuse suffered by aircraft on the flight and hangar decks (where they are constantly bumping into things) would also lead to a degradation of

the RAM's effectiveness. As a result of this quick look, the Navy decided against procuring F-117As and began the ill-fated A-12 program.

When the A-12 was cancelled in January 1991, Lockheed began to market an improved F-117 to the Navy as a replacement. This F-117N was based loosely on the second F-117B design, with a reduced wing sweep and long wing span. The outer wing panels folded to conserve deck space. Components from the F-14 were used in a strengthened landing gear, and a central keel provided a mounting location for an arresting hook. Various pieces of Navy avionics replaced their Air Force counterparts. The aircraft had a gross take-

off weight of 65,700 pounds. The Navy was not interested.

Lockheed tried again with the more radically modified A/F-117X. This design used afterburning F414 engines, and LPI radar, and could carry 10,000 pounds of payload internally, with four external hard points for an additional 8,000 pounds. The effect this had on the RCS was undoubtedly negative, as was the proposal to add a bubble canopy to improve visibility. An air-to-air capability was added through the addition of AIM-120 and AIM-9[8] missiles, although the aircraft was in no way intended to be a fighter. In 1995, Lockheed proposed converting one of the remaining FSD aircraft to the

F-117X SeaHawk configuration as a technology demonstrator, hoping for a contract for 255 production aircraft worth $3.1 billion. Again, the Navy was not interested.

An RF-117 reconnaissance variant for the Air Force would have used a side-looking electro-optical sensor in a ventral canoe that replaced one of the two weapons bays. The other weapons bay would still be available to carry the normal range of stores. No other changes were proposed, but apparently funding was not available to pursue the idea.

Lockheed has also made several attempts to interest the Royal Air Force in various versions of the F-117. Some of these were essentially the same as the F-117A except for the use of some British equipment, while others have run the gamut of modifications proposed to the U.S. Air Force and Navy. Indications are that some of these variants have also included such items as bubble canopies (also proposed on some U.S. Navy versions) and B-2 style compound-curved air intakes. Although the RAF has expressed some interest at times, nothing has ever come of the proposals.

As late as 1995 Lockheed was trying to interest the Air Force in an upgraded F-117A+ version. Lockheed proposed to convert a single aircraft to the new configuration for $79 million, but the Air Force could not find the funds to proceed and decided to adopt some por-

tions of the undisclosed upgrades piecemeal as funds permitted.

The total costs for the F-117 program have been released as just over $6.5 billion. Each aircraft cost $42.6 million, for a total of $2.5 billion for procurement. Development added $2 billion, and military construction amounted to $295 million. The cost of various upgrades account for the difference.

Training stores can also be carried in the weapons bays, as seen here. Note the small spoilers (squares with holes) that deploy in front of the weapons bays to ensure a clean airflow around the deployed trapezes. Originally all weapons were released with the trapezes fully extended, but subsequent testing showed that most can be released with the trapezes in the retracted position. (Skunk Works/Denny Lombard)

[1] David C. Aronstein and Albert C. Piccirillo, *HAVE BLUE and the F-117A – Evolution of the "Stealth Fighter"*, American Institute of Aeronautics and Astronautics, Reston, VA, 1997, p 141. [2] Jon Lake, *Lockheed Martin F-117 – Under the Skin of the Black Jet*, <u>AIR International</u>, August 1998. [3] Robert F. Dorr, *Lockheed F-117 Nighthawk*, World Air Power Journal Special, 1995, p 49. [4] Air Force News Service release "New, Improved Nighthawk Arrives at Holloman," 11 February 1997. [5] Jon Lake, *Lockheed Martin F-117 – Under the Skin of the Black Jet*, <u>AIR International</u>, August 1998. [6] Robert F. Dorr, *Lockheed F-117 Nighthawk*, World Air Power Journal Special, 1995, p 31. [7] David C. Aronstein and Albert C. Piccirillo, *HAVE BLUE and the F-117A – Evolution of the "Stealth Fighter"*, American Institute of Aeronautics and Astronautics, Reston, VA, 1997, p 128. [8] Robert F. Dorr, *Lockheed F-117 Nighthawk*, World Air Power Journal Special, 1995, p 49. [9] David C. Aronstein and Albert C. Piccirillo, *HAVE BLUE and the F-117A – Evolution of the "Stealth Fighter"*, American Institute of Aeronautics and Astronautics, Reston, VA, 1997, p 145. [10] According to Aronstein and Piccirillo, (page 144) there were plans to flight test both the AIM-7 and AIM-9 on the F-117A, and a static fit check of the AIM-9 was conducted sometime in 1982. [11] Jay Miller, *Lockheed Martin's Skunk Works*, Midland Counties Publishing, 1995, p 173.

The bottom of the F-117 shows the landing gear wells, and other details. The light line on the aft centerline is the tail hook (which is painted red). Various flush antennas can be seen, as can the retractable navigation light and UHF radio antenna. This aircraft (804) is wearing tail codes from the test group at Nellis AFB. (Tony Landis)

When the F-117A was unveiled to the press and public at Nellis AFB, armed guards surrounded the aircraft. The same was true of its initial airshow appearances, although by the late 1990s the guards were generally gone. Nevertheless, at most airshows the aircraft remains roped off, more to protect its delicate RAM than for security reasons. (Skunk Works/Eric Schulzinger)

Pilot access on the F-117A is generally via a large platform that also accommodates the ground crew that assists the pilot in strapping in. Special care is needed to ensure that the RAM is not damaged. The F-117A does not have built-in boarding steps like most fighters. (Skunk Works/Denny Lombard and Eric Schulzinger)

Every F-117A hangar has an American flag hanging from it, even when the aircraft is deployed to overseas bases. The hangars at Holloman are roomy and modern. Note the extensive lighting and ventilation systems. An in-ground fuel system allows the aircraft to be refueled in the hangar. (Skunk Works/Denny Lombard)

The relatively wide track of the F-117's landing gear makes the aircraft relatively easy to handle in cross-winds, and allows fairly high taxi speeds. (Skunk Works/Denny Lombard and Eric Schulzinger)

In recent years, the F-117A's intake screens have rarely been painted black – apparently it was a maintenance problem. As the aircraft moved out of the black world it received more informational markings (lift points, etc.) but still has relatively few compared to most other modern aircraft. (Skunk Works/Tom Reynolds)

When the F-117A moved from Tonopah to Holloman, the T-38s went along. They also received new paint schemes – overall gloss black. Reportedly this was because the Air Force directed that all support aircraft be painted the same basic scheme as the Wing's primary aircraft. (Skunk Works/Tom Reynolds)

The pilot of this F-117 is using the FLIR to look at the tanker, permitting a relatively rare view of the optics-side of the unit. Usually the optics are pointed rearward to protect them. Note the open refueling receptacle on top of the fuselage, and the spilled fuel behind it. (Lockheed Martin/Judson Brohmer)

WARBIRD**TECH**
S E R I E S

Like most delta-wing fighters (which it nominally is), the F-117A has a relatively high angle-of-attack during takeoff and landing. The extreme forward location of the cockpit affords the pilot good visibility despite the high AoA. (Lockheed Martin Skunk Works)

The F-117A is towed by standard Air Force tow vehicles, and uses a standard F-15 tow bar. Nothing special about this part of its operations. The landing gear configuration makes ground handling (turning radius, etc.) about the same as other operational fighters. (Skunk Works/Denny Lombard)

Another good view of the slotted exhaust nozzle. (Skunk Works/Eric Schulzinger)

The Skunk Works test aircraft shows the upper surface detail on the F-117. Note the exhaust configuration at the trailing edge of the fuselage. (Tony Landis)

Aircraft 839 deploys a beige braking parachute at Holloman AFB. The parachute compartment is slightly ahead of the vertical stabilizers, so the pilot has to be careful when taxing at low speeds to ensure the chute does not get tangled in the verticals. Normally the chutes are released at the end of the runway and ground crews pick them up while the aircraft taxies to the ramp. (Lockheed Martin Skunk Works)

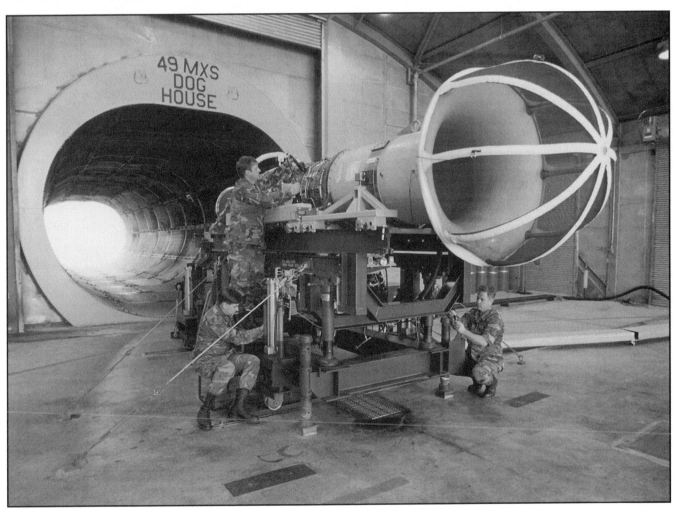

Maintenance technicians prepare an F404 engine for a static run in a test chamber at Holloman AFB. (U.S. Air Force)

The new hangars at Holloman AFB were built for the F-117A after maintenance problems were encountered by leaving the aircraft outside all the time. There is enclosed space for 40 aircraft. (Skunk Works/Denny Lombard)

This is not one of the new Holloman hangars. Note the illuminated light on the forward fuselage that is aimed towards the intake screen. (Skunk Works/Denny Lombard and Eric Schulzinger)

Unlike Tonopah, Holloman is an old and established Air Force base, complete with housing. In some ways it is an unusual place to locate the "secret" F-117 since it is also the location of the Luftwaffe flight school. Prior to the F-117A the primary American aircraft at the base was the F-15. (Skunk Works/Tom Reynolds)

Aircraft 835 at Holloman showing the new style tail code and serial number block on the vertical stabilizer. There is a great deal of debate over the use of fiscal years in the F-117A serial number since they appear to have been made up after the fact. (Lockheed Martin Skunk Works)

Aircraft 826 lands at Holloman. The pilot has not deployed the braking parachute yet, indicating this may be a touch-and-go landing. (Skunk Works/Tom Reynolds)

The F-117A was usually roped off from the public during air show appearances in the early 1990s. Even today this is often the case, mainly to protect the delicate RAM from prying fingers (Dave Begy via Mick Roth Collection)

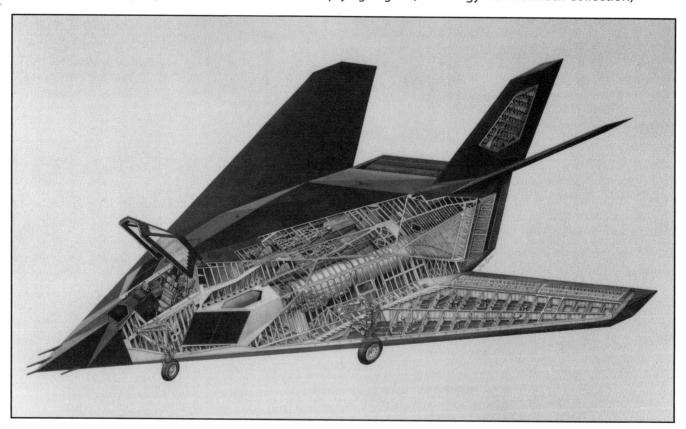

This interior diagram shows the position of the F404 engines in almost the center of the aircraft and the long tailpipes leading to the flattened exhausts. Fuel is in integral wing tanks. (Lockheed Martin Skunk Works)

STEALTH FIGHTER

DARKER THAN NIGHT

Lockheed seems to have developed a passion for black aircraft. The U-2, A-12, and SR-71 were all painted black for a variety of reasons. Even though it was reportedly an Air Force decision, the F-117 also ended up black. As a result, there is not much to show in a color section.

The two HAVE BLUE demonstrators at least were not black, and the first SENIOR TREND also appeared for a short time in other colors.

Then there was the red, white, and blue "American Flag" aircraft, which unfortunately was not extensively photographed, and unfortunately does not appear herein. It was reportedly spectacular, however.

Because of its multi-faceted design and black paint, the F-117 has proven more difficult to photograph than most aircraft – perhaps its designers also intended it to hide from the cameras?

The first HAVE BLUE demonstrator (right) was painted in the three-tone deceptive camouflage in an attempt to disguise its multi-faceted design. It reportedly was not terribly successful. The second aircraft (above) was finished in an overall light gray, most probably because this is the color the RAM came in. (Lockheed Martin Skunk Works)

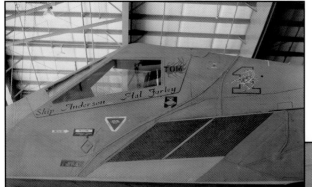

The first SENIOR TREND was later repainted into an overall light gray, and carried the scorpion marking superimposed on a 1. Note the lack of facets around the canopy – several FSD aircraft were finished this way since they were not intended to take part in RCS measurement tests. (Skunk Works/Denny Lombard and /Eric Schulzinger)

The first SENIOR TREND aircraft was also painted in a deceptive camouflage, although different than the one applied to the HAVE BLUE demonstrator. It also proved fairly ineffective. (Lockheed Martin Skunk Works)

The last F-117 Nighthawk is delivered to the U.S. Air Force during a gala ceremony – something that could not happen when the first aircraft was turned over due to security concerns. (Skunk Works/Eric Schulzinger)

WARBIRDTECH
SERIES

Exécutons.

An inert (notice the blue bomb casing – the color of inert weapons) 2,000-pound laser-guided bomb is dropped from a 49th TFW F-117A. The rear fins on the bomb have not fully deployed yet. (U.S. Air Force)

A 2,000-pound laser-guided bomb is loaded aboard an F-117A. The blue band around the bomb is another way of marking an inert round. Note the color around the exhaust nozzles and of the canopy glass. (Skunk Works/Denny Lombard)

Most F-117 missions are flown at night, and this is how the cockpit illuminates during those missions. The monochrome CRTs shown here have since been replaced by color multi-function displays which can also display the FLIR/DLIR imagery, freeing up the center CRT for use as a moving map display. (Skunk Works/Denny Lombard and Eric Schulzinger)

The F-117A cockpit is largely conventional in appearance and function, and uses components borrowed from other programs to save development time and funding. (Lockheed Martin Skunk Works)

TECHNICAL DESCRIPTION

For all the hype that surrounds the F-117A, it is still just a jet fighter, and not a terribly good one at that. Built strictly to exploit its stealth capabilities, it compromised many other areas of performance. It is worth noting that the F-117A was not built simply to defeat detection by radar. To quote Lockheed: "The F-117A employs a variety of design features to significantly reduce aircraft signature. There are seven different types of observable signatures of concern: radar, infrared, visual, contrails, engine smoke, acoustics, and electromagnetic emissions. The three signature characteristics providing the greatest potential for exploitation by threat systems are radar, infrared, and electromagnetic emissions. The F-117 is designed to minimize these signatures."

The overall shape of the F-117A is clearly a descendant of the original HAVE BLUE shape, which was a highly modified form of the Hopeless Diamond. It is a cross between a flying wing and a traditional delta, with no conventional horizontal stabilizers. There is not a curved surface on the aircraft, and each facet of its flat surfaces is angled in such a way as to provide the minimum radar return to the frontal sector. Radar absorbing material is used extensively to minimize the remaining signature.

It is worth noting that many photos of the F-117A do not show any radio antennas. This is because the four antennas are retractable, and are only deployed when needed. There are large blade antennas on the top and bottom of the fuselage for the voice radios, plus a transponder antenna and ILS antenna on the lower fuselage. Recently flush LPI antennas have been added on top of the fuselage for secure voice and data communications with satellites, U-2s, and AWACS. Detachable radar reflectors can be mounted on the fuselage sides so that local air traffic control can track the aircraft.

The pilot sits on a standard Boeing

There is nothing special about the flight garments worn by the F-117A pilots. The pilots sit on a normal Boeing ACES II ejection seat and look at conventional instruments and controls. (Lockheed Martin Skunk Works)

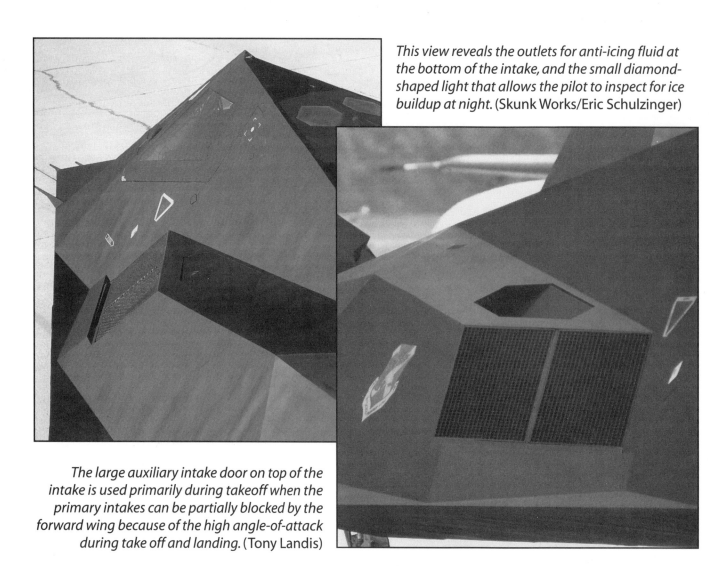

This view reveals the outlets for anti-icing fluid at the bottom of the intake, and the small diamond-shaped light that allows the pilot to inspect for ice buildup at night. (Skunk Works/Eric Schulzinger)

The large auxiliary intake door on top of the intake is used primarily during takeoff when the primary intakes can be partially blocked by the forward wing because of the high angle-of-attack during take off and landing. (Tony Landis)

(McDonnell Douglas) ACES II ejection seat, much like that found in any other Air Force aircraft. The current cockpit displays look much like any other modern fighter with two large color multi-function displays and a digital moving map display. One unique feature is a separate annunciator panel that lets the pilot know if any door or antenna is open or deployed, thereby compromising the aircraft's stealth characteristics.

HAVE BLUE had used a fixed-position side-stick controller identical to the one used in the YF-16 prototypes. Pilots found the fact that the side stick did not move at all (it simply sensed the pressure exerted by the pilot) rather disconcerting, so SENIOR TREND reverted to a normal center-mounted control stick. Interestingly, the production F-16 continued to use a side-stick controller, but one modified to move slightly in response to pilot's movements.

The cockpit of the F-117 is covered by a large hood-like canopy with five separate flat transparencies (one on either side and three in front). The canopy opens to the rear and has serrated edges in order to limit the radar reflectivity of the joint between canopy and fuselage when the canopy is closed. The five flat transparent panels are specially treated to further reduce the aircraft's RCS. The windshield is coated with a special gold film layer to prevent the pilot's helmet from being detected by radar.

The aircraft is not equipped with a radar set, relying instead on a unique adaptation of an off-the-shelf infrared acquisition and designation system (IRADS). Unlike most such systems that have a single FLIR installation, the F-117A needed two because of its unique shape and mounting requirements. One is mounted on top of the fuselage directly in front of the windscreen, behind a mesh screen to shield it from radar. The other is slightly ahead of and beside the nose landing gear door under the fuselage, and is called a downward-looking infrared (DLIR). Both turrets also include a laser designator. This installation was driven by requirements to see above the horizon, and also to see behind the aircraft

The F404-GE-F1D2 engine is essentially the same engine used by the Navy's F/A-18 without the afterburner. It is an extremely compact engine and has proven very reliable in service. (General Electric Aircraft Engines)

so that bombs could be followed after deployment. This involved some development effort to allow the two turrets to queue each other, and also to invert the video from the lower turret so that the perspective was correct when displayed. Despite this, the two turrets are largely identical and may be interchanged by maintenance personnel as needed.[1]

The F-117A is powered by two 10,800 lbf General Electric F404-GE-F1D2 turbofan engines without afterburners. The engines are essentially identical to the ones used by the Navy's F/A-18 Hornet except the afterburner has been deleted. Interestingly, the engines were ordered by the Air Force under an unclassified contract directly to GE instead of being procured through the Navy. The only restriction placed upon GE was that it would not directly communicate

The cockpit of the F-117 is conventional, with most of the major items coming from other programs, notably the F/A-18A. (U.S. Air Force)

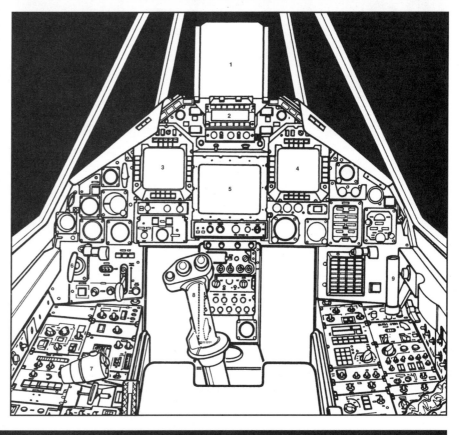

1. Heads-Up Display
2. Attack Profile and Autopilot Mode
3. Multi-Function Display
4. Multi-Function Display
5. IRADS (Replaced by Moving Map)
6. Emergency Gear Extension
7. Throttle
8. Control Stick
9. Canopy Locking Handle

with Lockheed, nor mention Lockheed or the SENIOR TREND program in any correspondence or open literature. These restrictions have been lifted.

The engines are fed by a pair of air intakes, one on each side of the upper fuselage. Two gratings with rectangular openings cover each intake to prevent radar waves from traveling down the intake ducts and reaching the engine compressor blades, which would tend to produce large echoes. This works because the spacing between the grids on the grating are smaller than the wavelengths of most radars. The small fraction of incident radar energy which does pass through the grating is absorbed by RAM mounted inside the duct, which does not curve or contain baffles. Airflow quality through the grids is surprisingly good. Although the grids create a slight pressure drop, resulting in some thrust penalties, they actually provide a very uniform pressure across the duct resulting in minimum distortion at the compressor face. The inlet grid pressure recovery is nearly constant for all angles of attack and sideslip.

Ice buildup on the intake gratings is a persistent problem, and the F-117 uses old-fashioned deicer fluid to remove the buildup. A light is installed on each side of the aircraft so that the pilot can visually check the inlets during night flying.[2]

One of the more unusual aspects of the F-117 is its engine exhaust system. Like the air inlets, the exhaust outlets are mounted atop the wing chord plane, one on each side of the centerline. Because of temperature considerations, the entire rear fuselage is constructed mostly of titanium alloys, the largest such use in the airframe. The engine exhausts are narrow and wide and are designed to present as low an IR signature as possible. In addition, they are intended to mask the rear of the engine from radar illumination from the back.

The exhaust ducts transition from the circular engine outlet to the flattened louvered exhaust ducts on the trailing edge of the fuselage, reportedly without seriously com-

According to Lockheed, the exhaust ducts were the single hardest item on the aircraft to develop. Judging by the number of problems with them during early operations, this was most probably true. The ducts not only hide the rear of the engine from radar, they also serve to cool the exhaust significantly to reduce the IR signature. (Lockheed Martin)

The rear fuselage is constructed mostly of titanium alloys. This photo shows the area before the exhaust ducts have been installed. The larger opening on the centerline is the braking parachute housing. (Lockheed Martin Skunk Works)

Aircraft 842 shows the flattened exhaust nozzle on the F-117A. Note the radar reflector on the side of the fuselage and the extended navigation light on top of the fuselage. (Tony Landis)

promising the thrust rating of the engine. At the end of each of the narrow slotted exhaust ducts, there are twelve grated openings, each being about six inches square. These grated openings help to reduce unwanted radar reflection from the rear and they provide additional structural strength to the exhaust ducts. The exhaust gratings are shielded from the rear and from the bottom by the F-117's platypus-shaped rear fuselage section. The extreme rear edge of the aircraft behind the exhaust slot is covered with heat-reflecting bricks. Parts of the ducts themselves are covered by tiles that are remarkably similar to the Space Shuttle tiles, protecting the nickel alloy structure underneath. In addition, bypass air from the engine is used to help cool the metal structure of the rear of the aircraft. The exhaust system is complex, incorporating sliding elements and quartz tiles to accommodate heat expansion without changing shape.

Lockheed reported that the design of this exhaust system was the single most difficult item in the entire F-117A project. There were early operational problems with the ducts, mainly fatigue cracking from the severe temperatures encountered during normal operation. In 1991, a decision was made to fit a modified exhaust system involving the use of new heat shields, better seals, new airflow paths, and new high-temperature thermal protection at the edge of the exhaust system.

The aircraft's thrust-to-weight ratio is only 0.4:1 at normal gross takeoff weights, barely adequate in warm climates and absolutely dismal compared with the nearly 1:1 ratio achieved by the more conventional F-15 and F-16.

The F-117A has six movable control surfaces consisting of four trailing-edge elevons which provide both pitch and roll control, and two ruddervators provide yaw control. The four elevons can deflect upward or downward by 60°, and the rudders can deflect 30° left or right. Like everything else on the aircraft, the control surfaces have a faceted design, particularly the ruddervators which use a flattened diamond cross-section. An unusual feature of the control surfaces, also seen on the F-22, are small flat-sided cutouts along the gaps between the surfaces and the main structure. These help disperse the radar reflections, especially when the surfaces are deflected.

The primary weapon of the F-117A is the laser-guided bomb (LGB). Two weapons bays are provided, and each can carry a single 2,000-pound weapon on a retractable trapeze. The trapeze is used to load the bombs, and was originally deployed below the bottom of the fuselage prior to dropping a bomb to ensure the weapon cleared the aircraft. Later tests revealed that most weapons can be dropped with the trapeze in the fully raised position, lowering the amount of time the weapons bay doors are open and the aircraft's RCS is compromised. Large single-piece doors cover each weapons bay. Originally the F-117A could only drop a single bomb at a time, but the OCIP I modifications removed this restriction.[3]

The two primary weapons carried by the F-117A are the GBU-10 thin-skin bombs used by most attack aircraft in the Air Force inventory, or the rather unique GBU-27. Either the 2,000-pound Mk 84 general purpose bomb or the 2,000-pound

BLU-109B deep penetrator may form the basis for either bomb. Smaller LGBs, such as the 500-pound GBU-12, were also carried by the F-117 during Desert Storm.[4]

Recently the F-117A has been cleared to carry both the AGM-154 Joint Standoff Weapon (JSOW) and the AGM-158 Joint Standoff Air-to-Surface Missile (JASSM).

The Raytheon (formerly Texas Instruments) AGM-154 JSOW uses a GPS/INS system for midcourse navigation and imaging infrared (IIR) for terminal homing. The JSOW is just over 13 feet long and weighs 1,000-1,500 pounds. The JSOW is being certified for use on the F-14A/B/D, F/A-18, AV-8B, F-15E, F-16C/D, F-117A, B-1B, and B-52H.

The JSOW provides a standoff

range of 17 miles for a low level release, and 46 miles for a high altitude release. The weapon can turn through 180° to engage off-bore-site targets. If released at high speeds, JSOW will delay wing deployment to avoid penalizing its range by drag. The weapon can also be programmed to attack a target from a specific heading, and to fly between multiple programmed waypoints. A typical profile is to glide in at an altitude of 200 feet, pop up close to the target and dive in to dispense its payload from several hundred feet.

The AGM-154A is intended for use against soft targets such as parked aircraft, vehicles, SAM sites, and mobile command posts. It carries 145 BLU-97A/B combined effects bomblets (CEB) which are deployed as the JSOW dives from medium altitudes. These are the same CEBs

A travel pod can be accommodated in each weapons bay, although since the F-117A is a single seat fighter, only one is generally carried. This 49th FW aircraft was photographed on 2 October 1992. (Don Logan via Mick Roth Collection)

that are used on the CBU-87 cluster bomb. Each CEB has a conical shaped charge which can penetrate 5-7-inches of armor, a main charge which produces about 300 high velocity fragments, and a Zirconium sponge incendiary element.

The AGM-154B is a specialized antiarmor weapon which carries six BLU-108/B sensor fuzed weapon (SFW) submunitions. These are the same SFWs that are used in the CBU-97 cluster bomb. Planned Air Force improvements to the SFW submunition will include a better IR sensor and a warhead which will produce a slug and a shrapnel pattern.

The total development cost for the AGM-154A version was $417.9 million, with a further $227.8 million being expended on the AGM-154B version and $452.4 million more on the AGM-154C. The unit costs of the three versions are $282,000, $484,167, and $719,012, respectively and total acquisition costs are $3,327.6, $2,033.5, and $5,608.3 million, respectively. The Air Force is currently programmed to acquire 3,000 each of the AGM-154A and AGM-154B models, and has ordered 193 in FY00.

The AGM-158 JASSM is a low observable air-launched cruise missile that provides a conventional launch-and-leave precision-guided weapon capable of operating in adverse weather. It has a range of 115+ miles and carries a 1,000-pound class unitary warhead. JASSM's midcourse guidance is provided by a GPS/INS protected by a new antijam GPS null steering antenna system. In the terminal phase, JASSM is guided by an IIR seeker and a pattern matching-autonomous target recognition

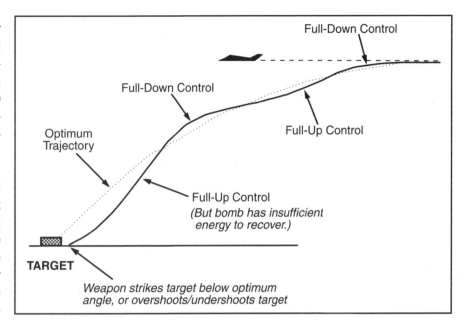

These two charts illustrate the difference in trajectories between the Paveway II (above) and Paveway III (below) LGBs. The Paveway II could only deflect its control surfaces full-up or full-down, which generally meant the weapon was not on its best trajectory. This frequently resulted in the weapon falling short or overshooting its target by a few dozen feet, or hitting the target at a less than ideal angle for penetration. The Paveway III introduced full-authority flight controls that keep the weapon closer to its ideal trajectory, greatly improving its accuracy and effectiveness. (U.S. Air Force)

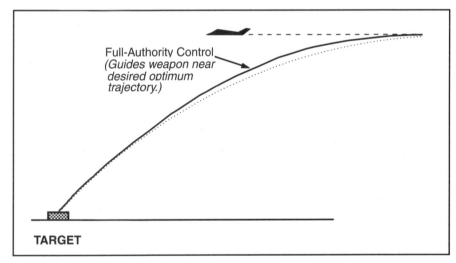

system. The JASSM is being certified for use on the B-1B, B-2, B-52H, F-117A, F-15E, F-16C/D, F/A-18, P-3, S-3, and the Joint Strike Fighter.

In early 1998, Lockheed Martin was selected as the JASSM production contractor and began delivering preproduction units for continued testing. The first 87 missiles were ordered in FY00, and the total production for the Air Force is expected to be 2,400 missiles; the total for the Navy is yet to be determined. The total program is valued at approximately $3,000 million. The program is emerging as a model for acquisition reform and the program office's objective is to keep the unit cost below $400,000 in FY95 dollars, with the threshold being $700,000. Estimates are currently at $300,000 per missile.

The conflict over Kosovo gave the Air Force the chance to demonstrate a new non-lethal weapon carried by the F-117.

The CBU-94 carries BLU-114/B submunitions in a standard SUU-66/B tactical munitions dispenser (TMD). This is the same basic dispenser used by most other cluster bombs in the U.S. inventory. The F-117A was modified during 1995 to carry submunitions based on the TMD.

Each BLU-114/B is approximately 10 inches high and three inches in diameter. When the clamshell doors of the TMD open at low altitude, the submunitions are dispersed by

One of the latest weapons to be certified on the F-117A is the AGM-158 JASSM stealthy standoff missile. A single AGM-158 may be carried in each weapons bay. (Skunk Works/Denny Lombard)

centrifugal force in a large circle. Each BLU-114/B is then stabilized by a small parachute, and spools of specially-treated carbon-graphite wires are shot out by small explosive charges to unravel and criss-cross into a web as they near the ground.

These wires land on high-voltage power lines, shorting them out and causing flash fires and large explosions of sparks. The resulting power surges cause powerplant circuit breakers to trip, shutting off the dis-tribution of electricity, but causing little permanent damage.

During the first raids on the night of 2 May 1999, over 70 percent of Yugoslavia lost power for several hours. Similar weapons had been used during Operation Desert Storm in 1991, but had used Tomahawk cruise missiles as delivery vehicles.

Although the original requirements called for the SENIOR TREND to be compatible with the B61 tactical nuclear weapon, as far as is known, no compatibility testing or certification was ever carried out with the weapon, and no controls exist for it in the cockpit. With the recent trend towards downplaying nuclear weapons capabilities, it is likely that this requirement was simply waived by the Air Force.

The F-117 is also not equipped to carry a gun, and as far as is known, cannot carry any air-to-air missiles, although some studies have been conducted into carrying AIM-9 and AIM-120 weapons.

[1] David C. Aronstein and Albert C. Piccirillo, *HAVE BLUE and the F-117A – Evolution of the "Stealth Fighter"*, American Institute of Aeronautics and Astronautics, Reston, VA, 1997, p 71. [2] *Ibid*, p 99. [3] Robert F. Dorr, *Lockheed F-117 Nighthawk*, World Air Power Journal Special, 1995, p 32. [4] *Ibid*.

The pitot probes proved to be one of the more difficult things designed for the SENIOR TREND program. The trick was to develop a probe with an opening large enough to provide good quality air data, but small enough not to be detected by radar at reasonable ranges. (Lockheed Martin)

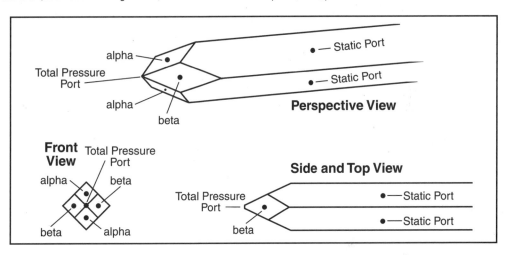

An AGM-158 JASSM is loaded aboard one of the test aircraft at Edwards AFB. (Skunk Works/Eric Schulzinger)

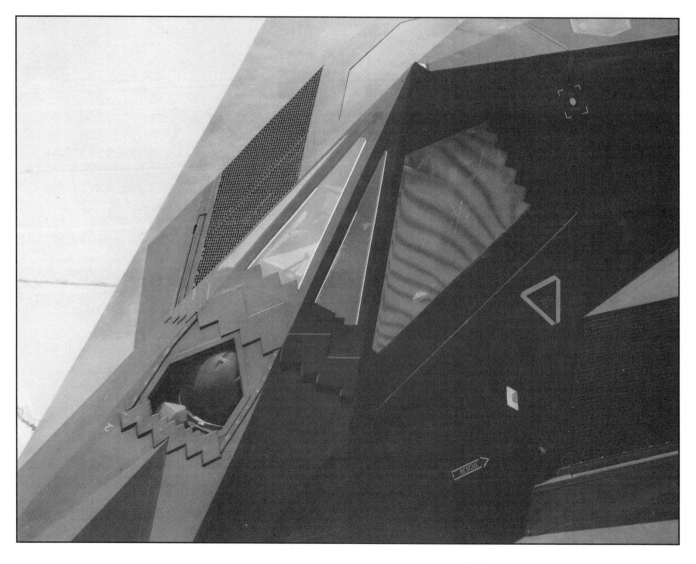

The faceting around the canopy and FLIR turret is evident in this photo. The FLIR turret is turned in toward the aircraft – its normal position to protect the optics. Only when it is being used does the turret face forward, exposing the IR sensor and laser designator. (Skunk Works/Eric Schulzinger)

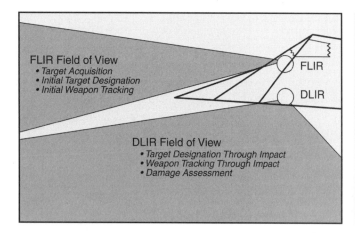

FLIR Field of View
- *Target Acquisition*
- *Initial Target Designation*
- *Initial Weapon Tracking*

FLIR

DLIR

DLIR Field of View
- *Target Designation Through Impact*
- *Weapon Tracking Through Impact*
- *Damage Assessment*

The placement of the FLIR turret dictated that a second (DLIR) turret was necessary to see under and behind the aircraft. (Lockheed Martin)

The LGBs need to have their target designated by a laser during their entire flight. The laser does not have to be from the F-117. (Mick Roth)

The F404 engine is typical of modern jet engines with a basically uncluttered external appearance. Without an afterburner attached, the engine is remarkably compact. (Skunk Works/Denny Lombard and Eric Schulzinger)

Laser-guided bombs being loaded on F-117As. Note the spoilers deployed at the leading edge of the weapons bays and the faceted leading edges on the doors. As video from Desert Storm and Allied Force has shown, the current generation of laser-guided weapons can be remarkably accurate, destroying a specific target without inflicting collateral damage. (Skunk Works/ Denny Lombard)

Even with all the advances in modern aircraft, loading weapons is largely a manual affair, although the hydraulic jack on this weapons truck makes lugging 2,000 pounds a lot easier. (Skunk Works/Denny Lombard)

A pilot inspects the exhaust duct of his F-117A before a flight. Note the old style serial number on the tail, and the unusual hinge line separating the ruddervator from the rest of the tail. (Skunk Works/Denny Lombard)

WARBIRD**TECH**
S E R I E S

This is the current style of serial numbers carried by the F-117A, implying that there was a fiscal year associated with the original Lockheed manufacturing number. The 49th OG markings and small HO tail code are unusual – normally a large HO tail code is carried. (Craig Kaston via the Mick Roth Collection)

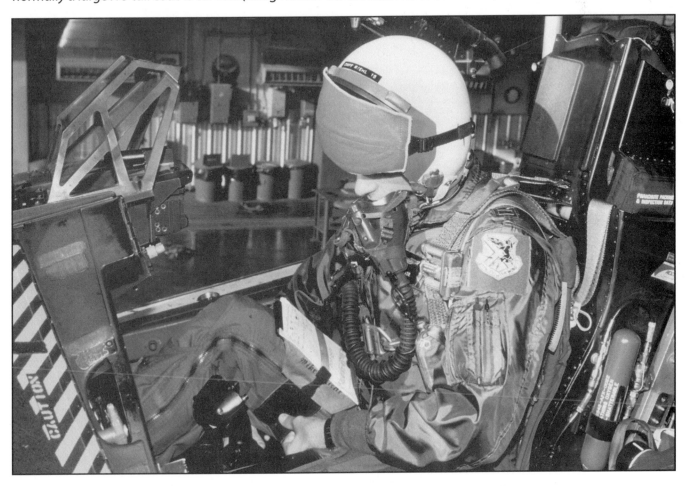

A 37th FW pilot preflights his F-117A. (Lockheed Martin Skunk Works)

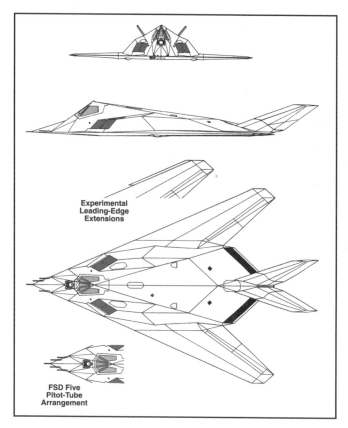

The remains of the first production aircraft form the basis of this display at Palmdale. (Mick Roth)

A three-view drawing of the F-117, with inserts showing the experimental LEX and FSD nose. (Lockheed Martin)

One of the FSD aircraft was mounted on a pylon at Nellis AFB after it was retired. (Mick Roth Collection)

An F-117A sports HO tailcodes in September 1993. (David F. Brown via Mick Roth Collection)

STILL A SILVER BULLET

The first time the Air Force apparently considered using the stealth fighter in combat was during the invasion of Grenada during Operation Nickel Grass in 1983. However, the operation lasted only a couple of days, and the combat debut of the F-117 was put off.

In October of 1983, the United States considered using the stealth fighter in a retaliatory attack on Hezbollah terrorist forces based in southern Lebanon in response to the destruction of the Marine barracks in Beirut. In anticipation of action, the 4450th TG at Tonopah was put on alert. Five F-117s were armed and had their INS systems aligned for attacks on targets in Lebanon. The plan was for these aircraft to fly from Tonopah to Myrtle Beach, South Carolina, where they would be put in secure hangars. They would then wait for 48 hours for the crews to rest before being given the order to take off for a nonstop flight to Lebanon. Secretary of Defense Casper Weinberger scrubbed the

entire mission 45 minutes before the aircraft were to take off from Tonopah for South Carolina.

On 25 September 1985, aircraft 781 lost one of its vertical stabilizers while flying performance and flying quality evaluations. The fin was lost following a pull-up maneuver at 10,000 feet, and was filmed by a chase aircraft. Major John Beesley successfully landed the aircraft, and was later awarded the Distinguished Flying Cross for his actions.[1] This incident finally forced a long-awaited replacement of the vertical stabilizers.

On 4 April 1986, during Operation El Dorado Canyon, the United States attacked Libya in retaliation for state-sponsored terrorism. During the initial planning for the raid, the use of the still-secret F-117

was again seriously considered. However, once again, the operation was short-lived and the F-117 was not used.

In spite of the extreme security, some bits and pieces of the stealth fighter story did manage to leak to the press. In October 1981, *Aviation Week* reported that an operational stealth fighter was in development. Several people reported catching some fleeting glimpses of a rather odd-looking aircraft flying at night out in the western desert. More and more reports leaked to the media, so that all through the 1980s it had been sort of an open secret that the Air Force was operating a "stealth fighter" which was invisible to conventional radar. However, questions directed to the Pentagon by the press about the stealth fighter

An F-117A from the 9th FS leads the "New Mexico Triad" formation over the Kuwaiti desert. The lower F-16C is from the 188th FS of the New Mexico ANG at Kirtland AFB. At top is a F-16C of the 523rd FS, 27th FW at Cannon AFB. (U.S. Air Force/SrA Greg Davis)

were met either with official denials or by a curt "no comment," which only served to whet peoples' curiosity even further.

Novelist Tom Clancy placed the stealth fighter (which he called the "F-19 Ghostrider") in a key role in his technothriller novel *Red Storm Rising*, published in 1986. The Testors model company released a plastic model kit which it purported to be "80% accurate" to the true configuration of the "stealth fighter."

In the meantime, training continued out in the Nevada desert. On 11 July 1986, Major Ross E. Mulhare flew into a mountain near Bakersfield, California, while flying the seventh production aircraft (792). Major Mulhare seems to have made no attempt to eject and was killed when his aircraft disintegrated upon impact. A recovery team was immediately dispatched to the crash site, and the entire area was cordoned off. Every identifiable piece of the crashed plane was found and removed from the area. The cause of the crash has never been officially revealed, but fatigue and disorientation during night flying has been identified as a probable cause.

On 14 October 1987, Major Michael C. Stewart crashed while flying aircraft 815 over the Nellis range just east of Tonopah. He too apparently made no attempt to eject, and was killed. Again, the official cause was never revealed.

These two accidents, along with a need to better integrate the still-secret stealth fighter into its regular operations, forced the Air Force to consider flying the aircraft during daytime hours. This would in turn force the Air Force to reveal the existence of the aircraft. This announcement was originally scheduled to take place in early 1988, but internal Pentagon pressure forced a ten-month delay.

On 10 November 1988, the long-rumored existence of the "stealth fighter" was finally officially confirmed by the Pentagon, and a poor-quality photograph was released. The stealth fighter was kept secret for over ten years, the security and deception being so effective that all descriptions which had "leaked" to the media were completely inaccurate.

On the same day, the Air Force confirmed that the official designation of the stealth fighter was F-117A, which surprised just about everyone. The official designation of the stealth fighter had long been assumed to be F-19, since that number had apparently been skipped in the new fighter designation sequence which was introduced in 1962. In addition, it had always been assumed that the designation F-111 had been the last in the old series of fighter designations which had been abandoned in 1962 when the Defense Department restarted the whole sequence over again from F-1. This led to a seemingly endless round of rumors and speculation about aircraft designation gaps and secret projects, which continue to the present day. If the stealth fighter was not designated F-19, then just what was

It is difficult to tell from this distance, but this posed shot shows four special tail markings for the commanding officers of each F-117 unit based at Holloman AFB. From the right is the 49th FW, 7th FS, 8th FS, and 9th FS. (Skunk Works/Denny Lombard)

F-19? If the F-117A was part of the old F-sequence, then what happened to F-112 through F-116?

Operation Just Cause

On the night of 19-20 December 1989, six F-117As were launched in support of Operation Just Cause, a U.S. attempt to oust Panamanian strongman Manuel Noriega. Two of the F-117As were apparently launched in support of a Special Operations mission to capture Noriega which was called off before the F-117As arrived over Panama. Two of the other F-117As had a dedicated strike mission, while the other two acted as enroute spares. As strange as it may sound, the dedicated strike mission was intended to bomb an empty field. The field was located beside a Panamanian Defense Force barracks near Ria Hato, and the bombing was intended to "stun, disorient, and confuse" the Panamanians.[2]

The F-117As departed Tonopah and refueled five times during the round trip. The two Rio Hato aircraft each dropped two 2,000-pound GBU-27A/B bombs with BLU-109B penetrating warheads, striking the empty field. The lead pilot for this mission was Major Greg Feest, who later commanded the first attack on Baghdad. The other four F-117As returned to Tonopah with their bombs.

Operation Desert Storm

On 21 April 1990, the Air Force publicly unveiled the F-117A at Nellis AFB. On 12 July 1990, just three weeks before Iraq invaded Kuwait, Lockheed delivered the 59th and last F-117A to the Air Force.

A month later the 37th Tactical Fighter Wing (TFW) began a very public deployment to King Khalid Military City near Khamis Mushait in Saudi Arabia. This remote facility is located 1,000 miles from Baghdad, and would quickly become known to the F-117 crews as "Tonopah East." This marked the first overseas deployment of the F-117A. They could not have picked a better, or a worse, place. The Saudi's had spared no expense when they built KKMC – it was a modern state-of-the-art defense base with hardened shelters that could each hold two F-117As, good runways, excellent self-defense capabilities, and modern dormitories. The bad part was that it is in the middle of absolutely nowhere.

Three F-117As return to Holloman after a training mission. The unique shape of the Nighthawk is unmistakable from any angle. (Skunk Works/Tom Reynolds)

By early October, the 37th FW was flying combat rehearsals named SNEAKY SULTAN. Plans were made – what targets would be attacked, the tactics, weapons, refueling assets, etc. As planning progressed, it became obvious that Baghdad itself was heavily defended, perhaps more so than any other place on the planet. Since it would be political suicide to have aircraft shot down over the Iraqi capital, a decision was made that only two types of weapons would be committed to attacking the city. The first would be ALCM and Tomahawk cruise missiles – nobody really cared if they got shot down. The second would be the F-117A – very few people believed one could be shot down.

On 20 December 1990, the unit at KKMC was designated 37th TFW (Provisional), and included most of the assets of the two operational F-117A squadrons (the 415th TFS "Nightstalkers," and the 416th TFS "Ghostriders"), as well as some assets from the 417th TFTS training squadron. On 16 January 1991, the United Nations' ultimatum to Saddam Hussein expired.[3]

Twenty-two minutes after midnight on 17 January, ten F-117As from the 415th TFS attacked a ground-controlled intercept (GCI) site at Nukhayb, two air defense control centers and the Iraqi Air Force Headquarters building in Baghdad, a radar facility at Alo Taqaddum, a telephone center at Al Ramadi, two telephone centers in Baghdad, an integrated operations center in Al Taji, a military facility in North Taji, and the presidential grounds at Abu Ghurayb.

Twelve additional F-117As (three from the 415th and nine from the 416th) repeated the strikes against the Air Force headquarters, air defense control centers and telephone exchanges in Baghdad, the Alo Taqaddum radar facility, military targets in North Taji, and targets on the Presidential grounds at Abu Ghurayb. New targets included the Salmon Pak troposcatter station, a television transmitter, a radio transmitter, and the Presidential bunker in Baghdad, the Rasheed Airfield, a joint operations center at Al Rutbah, a troposcatter station at

Two weeks after the Iraqi invasion of Kuwait, 21 aircraft from the 415th TFS stopped over at Langely AFB, Virginia, on their way to Saudi Arabia. The next day they flew a 14-hour nonstop flight to KKMC. Note the black braking parachute on the aircraft taxing in the foreground. (Lockheed Martin Skunk Works)

Habbaniyah, and the satellite communications terminal at Ad Dujayl.

A total of 29 F-117As hit 26 high-value targets during the first night of air war.

But all of the carefully planned tactics did not necessarily work. When multiple bombs needed delivered to a single target, the plan was for multiple F-117As to attack at one minute intervals. It was believed this was sufficient time for the dust from the first blast to disperse sufficiently for the next aircraft to find the target. But it was not enough for the antiaircraft fire to subside. Ten minute intervals became standard.

The F-117A effectively attacked Baghdad, although not as often as originally planned by the battle staff. Bad weather prevented many missions from dropping their bombs. The lack of radar on the F-117A became a handicap. But the strikes that did occur were precise. A single building in a block could be destroyed without inflicting serious collateral damage on the others. Later in the war, the F-117 became just another bomb truck, no longer striking high-value targets exclusively.

One of the most dramatic moments of the war was shown on CNN when a pair of F-117As attacked the Al-Kark tower in Baghdad. A single GBU-27 LGB penetrated halfway down the tower before exploding, snapping the entire building in half. Seconds later another GBU-27 hit the 12-story Baghdad International Telephone Exchange directly across the Tigris river. A minute later another F-117A dropped a pair of 2,000-pound Mk 84s onto the telephone exchange. Most of the building collapsed.[4]

The post-war analysis showed that 45 F-117As flew 1,271 combat sorties totaling over 6,900 flight hours. A total of 2,000 tons of bombs were dropped, with 1,669 direct hits and 418 misses. During the conflict the F-117A had a mission capable rate of 85.8%, about 4% higher than its normal peacetime rate (this was true of almost all combat types

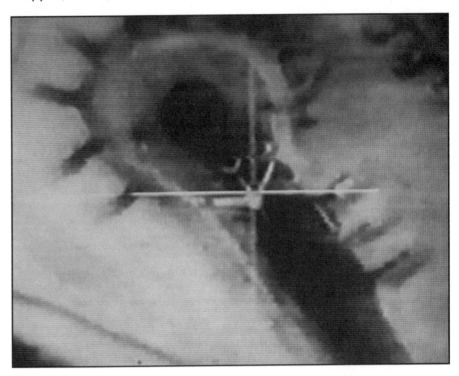

What a target looks like from the F-117 pilot's perspective. (U.S. Air Force)

Even in Saudi Arabia, the ground crew managed to keep their sense of humor. (U.S. Air Force)

An F-117 prepares to refuel from a KC-10 while deploying to Saudi Arabia during Operation Desert Storm. (U.S. Air Force/DVIC photo DF-SC-99-00066))

deployed). No F-117As were lost to enemy fire during Operations DESERT SHIELD or DESERT STORM.

From Tonopah

Beginning on 9 May 1992, the F-117A force began to move from their highly secret facility at Tonopah to Holloman AFB, New Mexico. This was largely an attempt to normalize the operations of the aircraft after it had received so much publicity. The 49th TFW at Holloman had operated F-15s for 14 years, the last of which departed on 5 June 1992. All three Tonopah-based F-117A squadrons (the 415th TFS, 416th TFS, and 417th TFTS) transferred their personnel and equipment to Holloman and became part of the 49th TFW. On 30 July 1993, the 415th and 416th were designated the 9th and 8th FS (the "tactical" having been dropped from the ACC's vocabulary). Six months later the 417th TFTS became the 7th FS, although its primary mission continues to be training.

Almost immediately various things conspired to disrupt the F-117As previously excellent readiness rate. Holloman did not have dedicated hangars available for the F-117As, forcing them to remain outside most of the time. This took a toll on the sensitive RAM. Many senior members of the maintenance team had elected not to leave the Nellis area (where they lived, commuting to Tonopah), depriving Holloman of a great deal of expertise. The remaining maintenance personnel were spread between Holloman and Saudi Arabia, where a contingent of F-117As was maintained to ensure Iraq did not attempt more tricks.

The effects were discouraging. The readiness rate, which had been averaging around 82%, dropped to 62%. The number of mission-capable aircraft went from 35 to 28 (out of 45 assigned). In 1994, the Air Force began to take action to correct the problem. It allocated an additional $174 million for facilities and parts, and assigned an additional 143 maintenance personnel to the Wing.[5]

The F-117A had always required more maintenance than most of its contemporaries. During its early career, the aircraft needed 150 maintenance man hours per flight hour, compared to 32.2 for the F-15A/B, 22.1 for the F-15C/D, and 19.2 for the F-16A.[6] Direct operating costs for the F-117A were roughly double those for the F-15 or F-4G, and three times those of the F-16A. By late 1989, thanks mainly to the availability of spray-on RAM, the F-117A needed only 45 maintenance man hours per flight hour. Still high, but acceptable given its unique capabilities.[7]

In August 1998, the Air Force reported that the total flight time for the F-117A fleet had surpassed 150,000 hours. The event was actu-

King Khalid Military City (or Air Base) was a modern installation with hardened shelters (above) each housing two aircraft. Note the rocks on top of the shelters, providing both camouflage and additional protection. The only serious drawback to KKMC was that it is in the middle of nowhere. In the photo at right, notice the articulating aluminum ladder instead of the large workstands. (U.S. Air Force)

Camouflage netting, the ever present American flag, and a bunch of civilian Lockheed workers surround this forward-deployed F-117 during Operation Desert Storm. (Lockheed Martin Skunk Works)

ally recorded on a flight conducted on 25 August by Brig. Gen. Bill Lake, Commander of the 49th TFW.[8]

A total of six F-117As had crashed between the first flight and the end of 1998. Two of these had been the result of incorrectly wiring the air data sensors, with the aircraft crashing immediately upon takeoff. Three others had been operational accidents during training missions. The sixth occurred during an airshow on 14 September 1997 at the Martin State Airport, Maryland. The pilot, Maj. Bryan Knight, ejected safely. The abandoned aircraft crashed into a housing development, injuring four people on the ground. The cause of the crash was later traced to missing fasteners that should have held the outer wing panel to

the fuselage structure. The entire F-117 fleet was grounded while Lockheed and Air Force technicians checked each aircraft, although no other anomalies were found.

Kosovo

The first combat loss of an F-117 (806) came at 12:33 am (local) on 28 March 1999 about 30 miles northeast of Belgrade during the NATO bombing of Yugoslavia. The pilot ejected safely and was rescued about six hours later by combat search-and-rescue teams using PAVE LOW helicopters.[ix] The name of the pilot was not released, although he was quoted by the Air Force News Service as saying "I knew I was fairly deep into Serbian territory. I had guessed my posi-

tion was within 20 miles of Belgrade – not a happy thought, considering the risk involved in a combat search and rescue that deep into Serbian territory."

The loss generated a great deal of initial speculation in the media about the effectiveness of the F-117A, and stealth in general. The Air Force declined to comment on the cause of the loss, leading to yet more speculation. The fact that the wreckage was not immediately bombed by Allied forces, a normal precaution when sensitive hardware is lost behind enemy lines, was blamed on an inadequate command-and-control system within NATO. Serbian television showed the wreckage the next day, and it is probable that Russian and

Iraqi engineers were allowed to examine it shortly thereafter.

The Pentagon countered that the F-117A represents the second generation of Stealth technology and is no longer of any great interest to Russia or other countries with the capability to manufacture a stealth aircraft. The Pentagon pointed out that the F-117A had operated over Iraq during the Gulf War without a loss, and was used successfully during the initial attacks on Yugoslavia when Serbian air defenses were considered their most effective. These comments led to speculation that the loss could have been caused by a mechanical failure or a lucky shot by Serbian defenses.

One senior official is quoted by *Aviation Week* as saying: "it appears that the F-117 was struck by a Russian SA-3 or SA-6 surface-to-air missile when the pilot dropped below 15,000 feet. That maneuver was necessary to get beneath clouds so that the aircraft's infrared targeting sensors and laser weapons could be used. The aircraft was then silhouetted against the clouds, detected visually, not by radar, and tracked by the air defense missile battery's electro-optical sensor."

Others sources dispute this and reminded everyone that stealth is actually low-observable technology, not no-observable. It is well-known that F-117s can be tracked by some types of radar given the right circumstance. They are also particularly vulnerable when they open their weapons bay doors since most of their weapons are not stealthy (not to mention the insides of the bays themselves).

Theories abound. One unnamed pilot speculated that the F-117A might have maneuvered to avoid a missile or other obstacle and suffered a loss of control, forcing the pilot to eject. The crash site was consistent with the falling-leaf way the F-117 tends to descend after a loss of control. Another official indicated that a "... known Russian radio-frequency jammer also could have interfered with the F-117 electronic flight control system ..." although this is thought unlikely. Still another pilot thought that the pilot might have ejected due to a malfunction. With the canopy gone, the RCS of the aircraft increases dramatically, allowing the Serbs to target the stricken aircraft, which ended up over 10 miles away from the pilot.

Serbian defenders had reportedly also been well briefed by Iraqi offi-

An F-117A deployed at Aviano AB, Italy, on 21 February 1999, just prior to beginning of the bombing of Serbia and Kosovo. (U.S. Air Force/SrA Mitch Fuqua)

Major Joe Bowley prepares to return to the United States after Operation Desert Storm. His crew chief, SSgt. David Owings, ensures that everything is ready before the pilot taxis. (U.S. Air Force/DVIC photo DF-ST-92-08445)

cials on lessons learned in the Gulf War, allowing the Serbs to predict some attacks, and to tune the radars more effectively to foil some countermeasures, although exactly what was done is unclear. It is interesting to note that the Iraqis claim to have tracked the F-117s late during Desert Storm. The only corroboration from the U.S. was that F-117 pilots saw Iraqi Mirages equipped with search-lights. The obvious inference was that something guided the Mirages close enough for the F-117 pilots to see them.[10]

Some officials contacted by *Aviation Week* also speculated that the Serbians may have installed a "first-generation stealth detection system" using multiple bistatic radars and modern computer algorithms. These systems have been proven effective on the drawing board by allowing multiple radars to receive the radar returns from each transmitter and triangulating the results. Nobody has so far announced the deployment of such a system, however the Russians do market a modification to a metric radar that they indicate gives the capability.

Another possibility mentioned in the Naval Institute *Proceedings* journal[11] is that the F-117A was tracked using an IR sensor. The theory is that the wings of the F-117 heat up due to aerodynamic friction and can be detected by a well-placed IR sensor. Since the Serbians knew the route the F-117 would most likely take out of the country, this theory seems plausible. It has been report-

ed that a B-2 was tracked during the recent Farnborough airshow by an IR sensor that detected the aerodynamic heat generated during the airshow performance.

A subsequent *Aviation Week* article shed more light on the loss, which was definitely caused by an SA-3 and not mechanical failure. The aircraft had completed its bomb run and was heading home. Apparently the F-117As had used the same exit route four nights in a row, allowing the Serbs to prepare. In addition, several SA-3 missile batteries had been moved, a fact not known to NATO planners before the mission. All of Serbia's long-range, low-frequency, surveillance radars had not been destroyed, and these are the radars most likely to detect an F-117.[12] The surveil-

Ironically, it was aircraft 806 that the Air Force featured in a photograph taken at Aviano just two weeks before it was shot down. (U.S. Air Force)

Serbian television was quick to show the remains of 806 after it was shot down on 28 March 1999, marking the first combat loss of the F-117. These photos show various pieces of the aircraft at the crash site. (Various Internet Sources)

lance radars had been picking up spotty contacts with the F-117As each night, and had pretty well defined their normal flight paths out of the country.

In addition, although U.S. doctrine states that even F-117As will have jamming support from EA-6Bs for every mission, the EA-6B on this mission was reportedly not in the optimum spot (although it was apparently in its assigned position) to protect the F-117A, being some 100 miles away.

Comments from the downed pilot indicated the aircraft was not directly hit, but suffered from a proximity explosion that damaged the engines and flight control surfaces. The pilot reported being buffeted by −5g after the explosion, making it difficult to eject.

Further details on the loss will probably not be known in the foreseeable future since it is unlikely that either the United States or the Serbians will break their silence to talk about it. It may have been a lucky shot by the Serbs, or it may have spelled the beginning of the end for stealth aircraft.

[1] David C. Aronstein and Albert C. Piccirillo, *HAVE BLUE and the F-117A – Evolution of the "Stealth Fighter"*, American Institute of Aeronautics and Astronautics, Reston, VA, 1997, p 147. [2] Jay Miller, *Lockheed Martin's Skunk Works*, Midland Counties Publishing, 1995, p 173. [3] Robert F. Dorr, *Lockheed F-117 Nighthawk*, World Air Power Journal Special, 1995, p 45. [4] Don Holloway, *Stealth Secrets of the F-117 Nighthawk*, Aviation History, 1998. [5] Robert F. Dorr, *Lockheed F-117 Nighthawk*, World Air Power Journal Special, 1995, p 48. [6] General Accounting Office (GAO), *History of the F-117 Program*, January 1990. [7] David C. Aronstein and Albert C. Piccirillo, *HAVE BLUE and the F-117A – Evolution of the "Stealth Fighter"*, American Institute of Aeronautics and Astronautics, Reston, VA, 1997, p 152. [8] Air Force News Service release "F-117 Stealth Fighter Logs 150,000 Hours," 28 August 1998. [9] Aviation Week and Space Technology, 5 April 1999, p 31. [10] Norman Friedman, *Serbian Air Defenses Take on Stealth*, Naval Institute Proceedings, May 1999, p 100. [11] *Ibid.* [12] Aviation Week and Space Technology, 19 April 1999, p 28.

A dozen F-117As were deployed to Kuwait in February 1998 when Iraq again defied U.N. weapons inspectors. (U.S. Air Force/MSgt. Greg Bade)

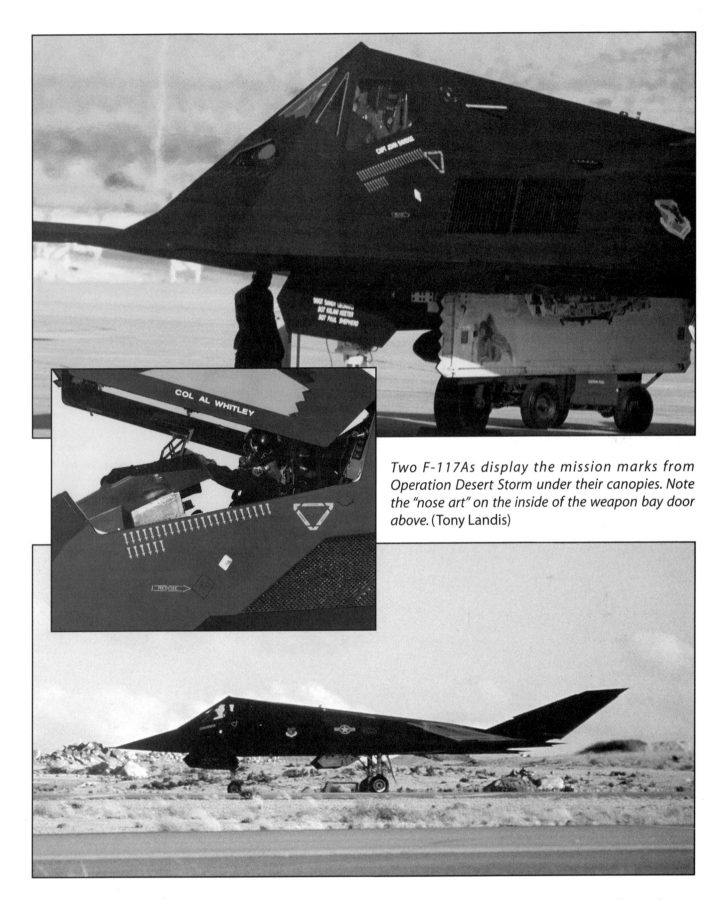

Two F-117As display the mission marks from Operation Desert Storm under their canopies. Note the "nose art" on the inside of the weapon bay door above. (Tony Landis)

An F-117A from the 37th TFW prepares to launch from an airfield in Saudi Arabia during Operation Desert Storm. (U.S. Air Force/DVIC photo DF-ST-92-08345)

An F-117 touches down at Aviano Air Base, Italy, on 21 February 1999 as tensions rise between NATO and Serbia. Note that the FLIR sensor is in the deployed position. (U.S. Air Force/SrA. Mitch Fuqua)

Displaying TR tailcodes from Tonopah and the old style serial numbers, a squadron of SENIOR TRENDs practices a deployment. Note the KC-10 in the background. (Skunk Works/Eric Schulzinger)

F-117s park along the Langley AFB flightline shortly after touching down on 19 November 1997. The aircraft remained at Langley overnight before leaving for Kuwait. (U.S. Air Force/SSgt. Vince Parker)

Using a black braking parachute, an F-117 lands at King Khalid Military City (KKMC) in Saudi Arabia in support of Operation Desert Storm. (Skunk Works/Eric Schulzinger)

SIGNIFICANT DATES

Early 1900s
James Clark Maxwell and Arnold Johannes Sommerfield develop formulae to predict the way any given geometric shape will reflect microwave energy.

1935
Robert Watson-Watt receives a patent for RADAR.

Late 1930s
The first radar-absorbing material is developed and sold commercially.

1956
Lockheed begins development of the A-12 – the first aircraft designed from the ground up to lower its radar cross-section.

1962
Piotr Ufimtsev publishes a paper on calculating the radar return of a two-dimensional object.

1974
DARPA contracts for various RCS reduction studies.

1 November 1975
Lockheed and Northrop are selected for Phase I of the Experimental Survivability Testbed (XST) program.

December 1975
Lockheed HAVE BLUE shape tested at Grey Butte.

April 1976
Lockheed declared winner of XST Phase I, and is awarded the Phase II contract.

16 November 1977
The Air Force selects Lockheed to develop the SENIOR TREND.

1 December 1977
First HAVE BLUE aircraft makes its maiden flight at Groom Lake.

4 May 1978
The first HAVE BLUE aircraft crashes on its 36th flight.

20 July 1978
Second HAVE BLUE aircraft makes its maiden flight.

11 July 1979
The second HAVE BLUE crashes on its 52nd test flight

18 June 1981
The first SENIOR TREND makes its maiden flight at Groom Lake.

23 August 1982
The Air Force receives its first SENIOR TREND (787).

10 November 1988
The Air Force publicly acknowledges the existence of the F-117 "stealth fighter."

119-20 December 1989
The F-117 participates in Operation Just Cause over Panama, marking its first combat use.

17 January 1991
The F-117 becomes the star of Operation Desert Storm, attacking targets in Iraq and Kuwait.

28 March 1999
The first F-117 is lost in combat during Operation Allied Force over Yugoslavia.

An F-117 undergoing heavy maintenance with the intake screens and canopy removed. (Lockheed Martin Skunk Works)